CRITICAL ESSAYS IN
MONETARY THEORY

CRITICAL ESSAYS IN MONETARY THEORY

BY

JOHN HICKS

OXFORD
AT THE CLARENDON PRESS
1967

Oxford University Press, Ely House, London W. 1

GLASGOW NEW YORK TORONTO MELBOURNE WELLINGTON
CAPE TOWN SALISBURY IBADAN NAIROBI LUSAKA ADDIS ABABA
BOMBAY CALCUTTA MADRAS KARACHI LAHORE DACCA
KUALA LUMPUR HONG KONG TOKYO

PRINTED IN GREAT BRITAIN

PREFACE

THE essays that are collected in this book, though they include two (or three) which will be familiar to many of my readers, and two more that have had some limited publication, are for the most part quite new work. I have chosen this manner of publishing them, in preference to the usual scattering of articles through journals, because I wanted them to be read together; and I have preferred it to the more consecutive treatment of a treatise or textbook, since I wanted each particular reader to read them in whatever order that reader found most inviting. They are the record of a process, extending over many years, by which I have at last formed my present conception of monetary theory. All the while I have been learning; as time has gone on, first one thing has become clear, then another. I have realized that truth is many-sided. Any uniform presentation could only be a photograph from one angle; by changing my approach I hope that I have achieved something more stereoscopic.

The nearest thing to a synthesis which I have been able to reach will be found in Essay 3, which appears as the third of those entitled 'The Two Triads'. The basic idea which is developed in that essay is very simple; but the reader will probably find that he has to consider it in the light of what is said in several others of these essays before he appreciates it fully. It depends, most directly, upon Essays 1 and 2, with which it shares a common title. These (1 and 2) are revised versions of lectures that I was invited to give at the London School of Economics, in January 1966; their then title was 'Foundations of Monetary Theory'. I did not publish them immediately, for I felt them to be incomplete. Later on (after I had had the advantage of discussing them with Professor Sayers and his seminar at LSE) I came to realize what it was that was missing. I had set up the columns on which the 'foundations' could be supported, but the cross-piece was still to be added.

I thought, at one time, that this book should just be a publication of the (enlarged) 'Two Triads', with no more added than the essays which here appear as 4–6, which might have been presented as appendixes. Essay 4 is simply a reprint of my old paper 'A Suggestion for Simplifying the Theory of Money' (1935). The relation between the doctrine of this paper and the Keynes doctrine (they are not, as often supposed, identical) is one of the matters that are discussed in the 'Two Triads'; so it seemed reasonable to put it in, as a document. Essay 5 (which appears here as 'The Yield on Consols') is based upon a paper that was given to the Manchester Statistical Society in 1958; I include it to show that I have given some attention to monetary facts, as well as theories! Essay 6 is a more conventional appendix; it may be regarded as a (rather more mathematical) supplement to the second of the Triad papers. It is an improved and much extended version of what orginally appeared as an appendix to a paper on 'Liquidity' that was published in the *Economic Journal* in 1962. (I have not reprinted the body of that paper, since almost everything of any value that was contained in it has been absorbed into the Triads.)

The question which runs through the essays in the second part of the book is of a different character. 'The Two Triads' is a revision and (perhaps one might venture to say) completion of Keynes's theory of money—by which I do not mean the whole of what is generally regarded as Keynesian economics, only his theory of money in a narrow sense. That is one of the things which has long been bothering me about the 'Keynesian revolution'; but there is another question also which I have found myself trying to answer—what kind of a 'revolution' was it? I made an early attempt to answer that question in my 1937 paper 'Mr. Keynes and the "Classics"', which is here reprinted as Essay 7. I have reprinted it here, because I felt that it was needed, though more for the essays which follow it than for those that precede it. As a potted version of the central argument of the *General Theory* it has been widely used (I have used it myself in that way in the concluding chapters of my book on the *Trade Cycle*). But as a diagnosis of the 'revolution', it is very unsatisfactory. It is not a bad representation of Keynes; but it does not get his predecessors (the 'Classics' as he called them) at all right. I have long felt that there was more to be said.

I made a second shot, using essentially the same diagrammatic method, in the course of what purported to be a review of Patinkin's *Money, Interest and Prices* (*Economic Journal*, 1957). It was not a good review of Patinkin; for I was unable at that time to formulate the basic reason why I differ from him, as I think I am now able to do.[1] The rest of the paper seems nevertheless to be worth preserving. Thus what appears here (as 8) is an abridgement of the 1957 paper, from which references to Patinkin have been omitted. I think that the paper is the better for the excisions.

What is given by this essay (8), even in its edited form, is the material for the revision that is called for, hardly yet the revision itself. For that task, which in this book is hardly more than begun, one must step back from one's diagrams; one must look at the history, and one must look at the texts. The general impression I have got when I have tried to do so, even only in terms of a few major authors, is set out, as simply as I can set it, in Essay 9. (This is the key paper in the second part of the book, as 3 was of the first. I dare say that there will be many readers who will find it the best place at which to begin.)

It is inevitable, when one tries to set a Revolution in perspective, that one should be impressed by the strands of continuity that run across it. (One can recognize these continuities, without denying the reality of the Revolution.) It is useful to recognize that pre-Keynesian monetary economics was not monolithic, in order to understand how it is that in

[1] See below, p. 52.

our day monetary economics is not monolithic either. Some of our present differences echo much older differences. There is one in particular, that came to the surface in the Currency School–Banking School controversy of the eighteen-forties (but is older than that), and which persists to this day. We still have a Currency School, seeking in vain—but one sees why—for a monetary system that shall be automatic. It is represented, over its long history, not only by Lord Overstone and his friends, but by Ricardo himself; not only by Mises and Hayek and Friedman, but also by Pigou.[1] The Banking School (or Credit School, as I wish they had called it) has a history of almost equal antiquity. It has greater names upon its roll than that of Tooke: Mill and Bagehot among the Victorians; Hawtrey and Robertson, as well as Keynes, in the twentieth century. The Keynesians, or followers of Keynes, with their fiscal policy, or monetary socialism, are one of the wings of the Credit party; but there is, and has long existed, another wing, which believes in monetary management, but also believes that it is necessary to be eclectic in the kind of management, and the means of management, that are to be used in each particular situation.

Henry Thornton (Essay 10) is the first great writer of the Credit School; though he wrote so long ago, he remains among the best. His values are different from those which are common nowadays; but his analysis is nearly impeccable, granted those values. We need him (and that is why I have introduced him here) to help mark out the field.

Keynes of the *Treatise on Money*, who was by no means a 'modern Keynesian', is also needed, in something of the same way. I have not attempted, in Essay 11, to write a full review of the *Treatise* (or even what Schumpeter would have called a Reader's Guide). I have confined myself to an

[1] That Pigou was at least at one time of that persuasion seems to me to be evidenced by 'The Exchange-Value of Legal Tender Money' (*Essays in Applied Economics*). At a much later date, his influence has been cast on the same side, through 'The Classical Stationary State' (*EJ*, 1943) and all its progeny.

attempt to help with some of the difficulties which inevitably confront the student when he turns to that book, and which stand in the way of his appreciating the splendid things that it contains. There are some quite simple things which need to be said. In the blaze of the controversy of the thirties no one seems to have said them.

One of the chief contributors to that blaze was Professor Hayek (*Prices and Production*). To one who like myself felt the full impact of that work on its first appearance, it has long appeared as one of the mysteries of economics. Something, one has long realized, had gone wrong with it; but just what? The question has been nagging at me; so I decided, a couple of years ago, to write out what I thought to be the solution. Wisely, as it turned out, I submitted it to Professor Hayek, who has turned from economics to social philosophy, but may sometimes be available for consultation. He told me, and he convinced me, that I had got him quite wrong. So I made another attempt, which appears as Essay 12 in this book. It is still something of an indictment, and I do not expect that Professor Hayek will plead guilty to it. But I think it is now clear of any straightforward misunderstanding.

The first of the acknowledgements that I have to make is to Keynes himself. His name, and his alone, appears in every essay in this book. I only just knew him personally; we had very little conversation on theoretical matters; I had a few letters from him that have helped me, but that is all. I know that he did read the things which I wrote, in his lifetime, about his work; I have taken account of what he wrote to me about them. Most of the Keynes that appears here is the Keynes of his published work, that is generally available to others. The rest is not much; but the influence, as a whole, is such that it must be mentioned first.

The other major influence which I have felt—less conspicuous, but no less real—is that of Dennis Robertson. In the twenties Keynes and he were close together; afterwards they seemed to draw apart; my own position (as the reader

will find it emerging, in bits and pieces, in this book) may
perhaps be somewhere between them. Robertson's influence
on me has been much more personal than that of Keynes;
from the time when we first met (in 1930) until his death in
1963, we kept up a running argument, sometimes on paper,
sometimes (whenever we met) by word of mouth. He kindly
referred to me, in one of his papers, as his 'mentor'; the
word would be more appropriately used by me of him. He
turned me back from several of the byways into which I
have wandered: over-emphasis on the 'speculative motive',
over-use of the Temporary Equilibrium method of *Value
and Capital*, to take two examples. He converted me to my
present insistence on the primacy of the Means of Payment function. Perhaps, from the point of view which I
reach in the course of these essays, I can look across at that
which he reached, many years ago, in 'The Snake and the
Worm'.[1]

Other acknowledgements (save one) are more special.
Those to Professor Hayek and to Professor Sayers[2] have
already been mentioned. My interest in the monetary writings, and in the monetary history, of the nineteenth century,
was first kindled while I was at the London School in the
nineteen-thirties—by the lectures of Theodore Gregory and
by many conversations with Lionel Robbins. It has been
maintained, over a long period, by my association, first at
Manchester, and then at our homes in the Cotswolds,
with T. S. Ashton. (A rather key point in Essay 9—one of
the last to be written—is due to a suggestion that was made

[1] Reprinted in his *Essays on Monetary Theory*; and again in the paperback *Essays on Money and Interest* (Collins, 1966) which I edited. For a
general survey of Robertson's work, see my memoir, which is prefixed to
the latter edition. The place when I am most consciously 'looking across'
is on p. 57 of this book.
[2] It should be said that my debt to Professor Sayers extends far beyond
that seminar, going back to the old days when we were colleagues at LSE
together. I have never been able to master the detail of monetary institutions; it has been an encouragement to me that Professor Sayers, who
does understand them, has usually found that in the general way I have
to talk about them, I am talking some sort of sense.

by Lord Robbins in his Chichele lectures at Oxford, in October 1966.)

I have finally to express my gratitude to the Warden and Fellows of All Souls College, for electing me (in 1965) to a research fellowship, of which the new essays in this book are, I hope, only the first fruits.

CONTENTS

1

THE TWO TRIADS · LECTURE I

WHEN the student is asked 'what is money?' he has still no choice but to give the conventional answer. Money is defined by its functions: anything is money which is used as money: 'money is what money does'. And the functions of money are threefold: to act as a unit of account (or 'measure of value' as Wicksell[1] puts it), as a means of payment, and as a store of value. With this traditional classification I have no quarrel whatever; I shall take it for granted in all that is to follow. But I want to go on from it to ask the supplementary question: what is the relation between this classification of function and that other equally famous tripartite classification, Keynes's three motives for holding money—the Transactions Motive, the Precautionary Motive, and the Speculative Motive? These also are reasons why (in some sense) money is required. We ought to be able to explain how the two triads fit together.

We shall not, I think, expect to find an exact correspondence. Keynes's classification is essentially 'close-up'; it refers to the behaviour of a single individual, or decision-maker, operating within a monetary system that is already defined. The other triad has a stance that is entirely different. It is most illuminating when we are standing right back, so that even the monetary system itself is allowed to vary.

When we stand back, not limiting ourselves to the monetary institutions of contemporary Britain or contemporary America, but looking about us so as to take account of other possibilities (such, for instance, as the monetary arrangements of Renaissance Italy, as described by Luzzatto[2] or by

---

[1] K. Wicksell, *Lectures on Political Economy*, vol. ii, p. 6.
[2] G. Luzzatto, *Storia economica d'Italia*, book ii, ch. 8.

Professor Cipolla,[1] or those of nineteenth-century China, as described by Dr. King,[2] the relevance of the functional classification becomes very evident. It at once becomes necessary to distinguish between a fully developed money, which possesses all three of the classical functions, and the various kinds of *partial money*, which have one (or two) of these functions but not all. The concept of partial money has hitherto been most at home in the interpretation of historical phenomena (as in the cases cited) but it is not in that light that I want to consider it here. I am going to maintain that it can also be used as an analytical instrument, by the aid of which we can explore some issues which still remain as dark points in monetary theory. One of the chief things which monetary theory ought to explain is the evolution of money. If we can reduce the main lines of that evolution to a logical pattern, we shall not only have thrown light upon history, we shall have deepened our understanding of money, even modern money, itself.

The first of the questions that can be approached by the use of a partial money model is that of the Transactions Motive—if it is a 'motive' at all, which we shall find reason to doubt. There is evidently a relation between the Transactions Motive and the function of money as a means of payment. What we shall require for this purpose is a model of partial money, which concentrates attention upon the payment function.

Money as a means of payment—or medium of exchange

Why do we require a means of payment? The textbook answer is that it is needed in order to facilitate multilateral exchange. Exchange which is confined to two commodities can take place by simple barter; but as soon as more than two commodities are to be traded, something in the nature of money is required.

---

[1] C. Cipolla, *Le avventure della Lira* (Milan 1958).
[2] F. H. H. King, *Money and Monetary Policy in China 1845–1895* (Harvard 1965), esp. ch. 1.

That makes sense; yet (as Patinkin[1] has shown us) it does not square at all easily with the theory of multilateral exchange, such as has been accepted by economists since Walras.[2] For although Walras does take one of his n commodities as numéraire (or unit of account) it is an essential part of his theory that the numéraire does not enter into the exchange in any different way from any other of the commodities. Any of the other $n-1$ commodities might have been taken as numéraire; all that would then have happened would have been that the $n(n-1)$ price-ratios between the commodities, taken pair-wise, would have been reduced to a basic $n-1$ price-ratios, by a purely arithmetical process, in a different way. The numéraire is not money; it is not even a partial money; it is not even assumed that it is used by the traders themselves as a unit of account. It is not more than a unit of account which the observing economist is using for his own purpose of explaining to himself what the traders are doing.

When this is realized, we can, of course, follow Patinkin and introduce a fully fledged money quite explicitly; but to add a 'demand for real balances' on the same level as the demand for commodities for want-satisfaction, seems to me to do no more than cut the knot. I prefer to proceed more slowly. I shall begin by constructing a model to which, in other respects, the Walras theory ought to apply exactly. I shall then ask how that model is to be developed, in order that a money, *which is to be no more than a means of payment*, is to be fitted in.

We should thus consider what would be the working of a market, on which a number of traders meet to exchange a variety of goods: a market which is only to be open on a particular 'day', so that it can be studied (as Walras studies it in his theory of exchange) in complete isolation from what went before and what is to come after. If we want to visualize it, we can think of it as one of those great fairs, which

[1] D. Patinkin, *Money, Interest and Prices* (2nd edition 1965), chs. 1–3.
[2] L. Walras, *Elements*, part iii.

played so important a part in the organization of trade in the Middle Ages; or indeed (except in so far as scale is a matter of importance) as the kind of weekly or monthly market which survives in country places all over the world. There are in fact several ways in which such a market could be conducted; and from the point of view of monetary theory (though not essentially, as we shall see, from the point of view with which Walras was concerned) it is essential to distinguish between them.

Indirect barter and commodity money

The first of these methods is that which I shall describe as *indirect barter*. Simple barter is not an allowable method; for if the only exchanges that are made are those which can be made under simple barter, the opportunities for advantageous trade will not be exhausted, and the market will (in general) fail to settle down to a Walrasian equilibrium. It will be no more than a collection of isolated exchanges; it is not, in the strict sense, a market at all.

It begins to move towards being a market as soon as some traders start to practise indirect barter. That is to say, they acquire commodities, not because they have a direct want for those commodities, but because they propose to exchange them, at a second round, for commodities for which they do have a direct want. It is tempting to say that as soon as this happens, we already have something which partakes of the nature of money—commodity money. But that is rushing on too fast. There is a further step which must be taken before we have a money commodity. All that has occurred, so far, is that some of the traders have started to act as middlemen; the commodities in which they operate may be quite different, as from one middleman to another. Even at this point some exchanges will become feasible which were not feasible under simple barter; but there is still no reason, in general, why the full Walrasian equilibrium should ultimately be approached.

For all that need have happened, while indirect barter remains at this rudimentary stage, is that market transactions have begun to coagulate into little knots of triangular trade, knots that need not be in any contact with one another. In order that the market should be *completed*, the knots must be brought into contact. More precisely, what this means is that traders must begin to acquire commodities, not for their own use, nor in order that they should be disposed of to others who have a direct use for them, but in order that they should be disposed of to other middlemen, who are prepared to accept the same commodity as an intermediary commodity. The intermediary is accepted, because it is known to be acceptable to others as an intermediary. It is at this point, I think we shall agree, that the intermediary commodity begins to partake of the nature of money. (Money is money, because it can be spent in the shops.)

Even so, it would be by no means necessary that the same 'money' should be used throughout the market. Different moneys might be used in different sectors; in order that the market should be completed it would be necessary that the sectors should be brought into contact—by the operation of some middlemen who act as 'money-changers', in effect using more than one of the 'local moneys' as intermediary commodities. When all the local moneys have been brought into contact, the market is completed; all the exchanges which are advantageous in the Walrasian equilibrium can in fact be made.

Granted these conditions, the market will in fact finish up in a Walrasian equilibrium. At the end of the 'day' (we are still considering a market that is confined to the single day) every trader will have reached a position in which no further transaction is open to him that can be carried through with the consent of other parties. The actual distribution of goods in that final equilibrium may indeed depend upon the income effects of trading that has taken place on the way, in the manner that is familiar. But it will be unaffected (save possibly through these same income effects) by the particular choice of commodities, to serve as intermediary commodities, that has been made in the course of trading. As long as the single 'day' is considered in isolation, the final equilibrium is determined by the supplies of commodities and by the utility-functions of the traders, just as Walras says. The numéraire does not come into it. It is just *our* numéraire, by which *we* describe the market equilibrium; it is just that and nothing more.

The point may be confirmed by observing that the organization I have just been describing—indirect barter completed by arbitrage transactions—is by no means the only way in which a multiple exchange market can be made to work. It is indeed a rather cumbrous type of organization. A market in which many goods had actually to change hands, not in order that they should be transferred from original supplier to ultimate demander, but because they were needed to serve as intermediary commodities, would be an inefficient market; but how can it be an inefficient market, when it has just been shown to finish up in a Walrasian equilibrium? There is a gap in the analysis of it which we have so far been giving; a gap that must be filled before going further.

It is implicitly assumed, in Walrasian analysis, that there is no cost (in terms of effort and sacrifice) in the making of transactions: but this, though a fair simplification for many purposes, is hopelessly misleading when our subject is money. Even the simplest exchanges are in fact attended by some cost. The reason why a well-organized market is more efficient than a badly organized market (even if the latter is a *complete* market) is that in the well-organized market the cost of making transactions is lower.

There are some kinds of transaction cost which can be admitted into the Walras model without making any great formal change;[1] if the cost is proportional to the volume of the transaction it is the same as if the transaction were subjected to a tax. (Actual taxes are, of course, an important element in

[1] If we allowed for economies of scale in transaction cost, a more serious modification of the Walras model would be required. My neglect of such economies in these lectures (I have quite enough to discuss without them) does not imply any doubt about their importance, nor of their high relevance to some parts of monetary theory.

transaction costs, in the real world.) As a result of the tax, exchanges will be taken less far than they would have been without it; and some potential exchanges will be altogether prevented from occurring. But the equilibrium which is reached will still be a Walrasian equilibrium, though a Walrasian equilibrium after tax.

As soon as transaction cost is allowed for, it becomes apparent that indirect barter (if it involves the actual physical delivery of commodities not ultimately required by the recipient) is in principle a costly way of organizing a market; there should therefore be an incentive to find ways by which this transaction cost can be reduced. There is the same incentive to find ways of reducing transaction costs as of reducing other costs; one way of looking at monetary evolution is to regard it as the development of ever more sophisticated ways of reducing transaction costs. Some of these can be found within the system of indirect barter. Standardization upon one commodity (or on a small number of commodities) to serve as intermediary; the selection of such commodities to serve as intermediaries as can be transferred at the lowest cost; these are obvious examples. By and large, the whole history of gold and silver money is no more than a set of variations on this theme.

The clearing system

There are, however, more thoroughgoing methods. It is possible to abstain altogether from taking delivery of intermediary commodities; so that costs of delivery are not incurred until there is to be a delivery from original supplier to final demander. It is indeed clear that all that has to be transferred, on the way, is a title to ownership. That applies, of course, not only to those goods which by becoming *generally* acceptable are already to be regarded as money commodities, but to all goods that are intermediary, in the sense of changing hands more than once. Actual trading need involve nothing more than exchange of titles.

There is, however, a distinction between a title to ownership, which is desired because it is to be exercised, either by the existing holder or by someone to whom he transfers it, as giving a right to disposal over some particular good, and a title which is desired solely because it is generally acceptable, so that it can be passed on. The latter may refer to one of the goods that are the objects of the multilateral exchange, or it may not. It could in principle refer to a real good, but to one that was not an object of exchange on this particular market. Or it may have ceased to refer to a real good altogether. In our Walrasian market all titles are to be cleared, at the end of the day; the fact there is no commodity which corresponds to the *abstract* money, that is now practicable, will not matter—if the titles to it can in fact be cleared.

There does indeed appear to be some evidence[1] that there were markets which operated, more or less in the manner that we are here contemplating, even among the medieval fairs to which I was alluding; but it is not for that historical reason that I wish to consider it here. It is one of the standard cases which a general theory of money ought to be able to cover; a limiting case, maybe, but a limiting case of quite crucial importance.

In such a market, A just sells to B against B's promise to pay, B to C against C's promise to pay, and so on. There must be some unit of account in which the promises to pay are expressed (a *partial money* of a different kind from that which we have been discussing) but that unit of account is not a means of payment, nor is it an object of exchange at all.

How would such a market work? It can work, but for it to be able to work institutions are necessary. There must, on the one hand, be a Clearing House where the debts can be cleared against one another; and it seems also to be necessary that there should be some arrangement which provides a guarantee against uncleared debts. It might seem at first sight as if such a guarantee would be provided automatically

[1] A. P. Usher, *The Early History of Deposit Banking in Mediterranean Europe* (Harvard 1943), ch. 4.

if the market were (as we have been supposing) genuinely self-contained in time, so that debts could not be carried forward; for to any uncleared debt there must be an uncleared credit, and it would be irrational to carry forward a credit which would necessarily become valueless as soon as the market closed. But reflection indicates that on a market with flexible prices (as such a market must clearly be) this is not quite sufficient. For suppose that when the debts are cleared, everyone is in balance except for two parties, A and B. A is debtor, B creditor. It is not necessary that A's debt should originally have been a debt to B; but when the debts are cleared, it must be converted into a debt to B. Now, as has been said, B cannot carry forward his claim; it must therefore be expected that he will try to realize it. There is, however, no reason why the commodities that A has acquired, or is left with, should be commodities which B desires to purchase; even if they are, when the market (on the point of closing) is confined to these two parties, there is nothing that will automatically prevent A from fixing an exorbitant price, so as to acquit his debt to B with what in real terms is a mere trifle. Thus while credit balances do automatically tend to remove themselves (when they cannot be carried forward) the same is not equally true of debit balances. If the market is to end smoothly, in a Walrasian equilibrium, some sanction against the abuse of debt facilities is required.

A market which worked in this manner must accordingly be an 'organized' market; it would require, at the least, a clearing house and something like a court of justice to make it work. These could not be established without cost. But this cost (which might be charged up as an entry fee to the market) might well be less than the cost of numerous cross-deliveries. If the only alternative is indirect barter, this 'clearing system' may be a viable type of organization. It is not a common type; but it deserves to be kept in view for the sake of its theoretical importance.

For it is with this organization that we first meet a clear case of the Wicksellian phenomenon, a market in which absolute prices—money prices—are indeterminate. The money is simply a unit of account; it is not one of the traded commodities; there is therefore no supply–demand equation to determine its value. The Walras equations are sufficient to determine relative prices, prices (that is) in terms of one of the traded commodities taken as numéraire; but this numéraire is not the money in terms of which calculations are made. That money does not enter into the Walras equations; it is altogether outside them. The money prices can be at any level, yet the same Walras equilibrium will be attained.

There must, however, be some level of money prices in such a market; and there must be something that causes it. We may perhaps get a hint from that alternative expression of Wicksell's which I quoted: instead of saying 'unit of account' he says 'measure of value'. It is inevitable, even in a market of the kind we are discussing, that the seller, when he is deciding whether or not to sell (or how much to sell) at a particular price, should implicitly consider what that price may be worth in terms of other goods; he must have some idea about other prices before he can say whether or not a particular price-offer is acceptable. It seems to follow that the level of absolute prices, on a particular day, will be much affected by what traders think to be 'normal'—by price-expectations which, even on a market in which the trading is self-contained, must be supposed to be based in some way on previous experience. (Even if we take it that no goods are carried over, we need not deprive our traders of *memory*.) Such price-expectations are, however, at the best, an insecure anchor; even though the memory of previous trials is carried over, it is probable that the absolute price-level will slip about, from one 'day' to another, in an undependable manner.

The banking system

I pass to a third type of organization, which may be called the Banking System. This is very like the Clearing System, save that the clearing house is replaced by a financier, or banker. (There need not, of course, be only one banker in the market; but we will begin by supposing that there is only one.) All of the debts which arose would then be debts from or to the Bank. Every transaction involves three parties, buyer, seller, and banker. After the first transaction, at the commencement of the day, goods will have changed owner-ship from B to A; A is left with a debt to the Bank, B with a credit. Since all debts are debts with the Bank, the clearing is automatic; and the enforcement of the balancing, at the close of the 'day' (we are still supposing that no debts can be carried forward) becomes the Bank's business. It is easy to see that a smaller degree of mutual confidence is implied in this arrangement than is implied in the Clearing System; and there are other ways in which it is likely to be more economical. It is not surprising that it is this kind of system which, in historical experience, has on the whole won out.

How should we interpret this arrangement in terms of Walrasian theory? It is tempting to say that bank credit has now become *money*; that it is both a measure of value and a means of payment; so that (apart from the limitation to the single day, which we are retaining, so that the 'store of value' function is still in abeyance) it is almost a fully de-veloped money. To such money it is tempting to attribute a Transactions Demand, so that one rushes on to a Cam-bridge Quantity Equation ($M_1 = kY$) or some equivalent. But there is not yet any demand to hold this money. It is not evident that anything has happened to make this model work any differently from the Clearing Model.

At the beginning of the day, none of the traders is in debt or in credit with the Bank. At the end of the day, the same is true. The 'volume' of bank credit builds up while the sales are proceeding (just as the volume of trade credit did in the other case); but it still sinks back to zero at the end. There is still no money outstanding when the market reaches its final equilibrium.

On the average, over the day, money is indeed outstanding.

We can add up the credits which the traders have at the Bank, and call the total the 'volume of bank deposits'. But this volume is entirely a matter of the volume of trading which is being done, and of the pattern (strictly speaking, the order) in which it is being done; it is not determined, like the *real* elements in the system, by the want-functions of the traders. In the final position, which *is* determined by the want-functions of the traders, the volume of money is zero.

I concluded, when considering the market that is organized on the clearing system, that the level of prices was in principle indeterminate. Are things any different here? Evidently there is no difference, if the Bank is prepared to meet any 'sound' demands that are made upon it. If the Bank adopts a purely passive policy, simply adjusting its advances to the 'legitimate' needs of business, it can have no influence upon the level of prices; all is as before. Nor is there necessarily any difference if the Bank becomes more restrictive. We must, in any case, be supposing that it is charging a fee (hardly yet interest, for the length of time for which the advance is to be outstanding will still be negligible); there must be a fee, which would naturally be charged as a percentage commission, to cover costs of administration. If it raises its percentage, the main thing that will happen is that the volume of trading that is financed by bank advances will be restricted; some of the exchanges which would have been advantageous if the charge for finance had been lower, will cease to be advantageous. Nothing to anchor the price-level will have been provided.

But what (it will naturally be asked) if there is a quantitative restriction of credit? It is arithmetically evident that if the whole of trade has to be financed by bank credit, and the order in which transactions have to be performed is fixed, a given volume of trade, at given prices, requires a determinate volume of bank credit. Thus if bank credit is reduced below the volume which is appropriate to the trade that is going on at the moment, something will have to give. Either prices must fall, or the volume of trade must be reduced, or there must be an adjustment in trading practices. It is natural to expect, in the general case, that there would be some effect at each of these margins. There would be some fall in prices, since some traders, being unable to dispose of their goods at the prices which would have been available to them if there had been no credit restriction, would be likely to lower the prices which they would be willing to accept. But there would also be a fall in the volume of trading; and there would also be some substitution of trade credit for bank credit (which may simply take the form of delaying payment). There is no reason to expect that the whole effect would be exerted in the form of a price-fall. Thus it is still true, even under credit restriction, that there is no firm relation between the volume of credit and the price-level; there is still no 'anchor'. It is perfectly possible, if price-expectations (or price-ideas) are unaffected by the action of the Bank, that the level of prices may be unaffected. Traders will indeed be obliged to accommodate themselves to the restriction of credit; but they can accommodate themselves in other ways.

It must further be emphasized that these effects—which are readily recognizable effects—work only one way. The Bank has two alternatives that are open to it—to restrict or not to restrict. By restricting, it can enforce contraction; but by not restricting—so long as it is doing no more than supplying a means of payment—it does not enforce expansion. When it is not restricting, prices are indeterminate; they may rise or they may fall. When it is restricting, beyond the market's requirement, prices (or quantities traded) will have a tendency to fall. If it is to keep 'control' without deflating, it must restrict without over-restricting; it must resist unwanted expansions without enforcing contractions. But that, it is only too obvious, is a razor-edge.

In order that such control should even be possible, there must be centralization of banking; either there must be just one bank, or one Bank that has control over other banks. A number of banks, acting independently of one another, cannot enforce a quantitative control. But if there are several banks, inter-bank debts (as well as debts between banks and traders) will have to be settled; they can be cleared through a Clearing House, or transferred to a Central Bank. If there is a Central Bank, it can (in principle) exercise the control. All this, it will be noticed, can already be said before we have left our 'means of payment' model.

The 'Transactions Motive'

The point is, however, approaching when we must leave that model, and prepare ourselves to begin at the other end, with the 'store of value'. The main conclusions which I propose to draw will depend upon that other inquiry, as well as on this; but it may be that even already I have enough to present an interim report. There is at least one result, with far wider application than to the world of the preceding exercise, which does seem to stand out. Even before going further, I think I should give it.

The analysis of the isolated market, operating upon its single 'day', can, of course, be no more than a preliminary to the study of a real economy. An actual (continuous) market will never settle down to 'equilibrium' in the way our 'single-day' market has been doing; but it is not unlike an echelon of such markets, one beginning and one ending at every 'hour', so that the later are still open when the earlier is closing. In such an echelon, there would always be money (for instance, bank money) outstanding, even if the closing of accounts, as each participant finished his business, was scrupulously maintained. But it could not be said that there was a 'demand for money for transactions purposes' in the sense of a voluntary demand, like the demand for commodities, which could be forced—even with an effort—into the mould of marginal utility theory. There would indeed be a volume of money outstanding (it might well be a fairly constant volume of money) but how much it was would depend upon the pattern of transactions conducted, not upon any individual decisions, not even upon any aggregate of individual decisions. For in its nature it is a disequilibrium, not an equilibrium phenomenon. And this seems to mean that we must expect it to be rather impervious to direct economic *incentives*.

It does seem to me that there is in practice a good part of the money supply (almost however defined) which in normal conditions is occupied in just this manner. It may even be that it is quantitatively much the larger part (though that depends on just what we are including in *money*). Statistical investigations (such as those made by Friedman and his collaborators)[1] which purport to show a regularity in the proportion between the value of income—or of transactions—and the total money stock, do to my mind (so far as they are successful) show no more than that the proportion of the total stock that is absorbed in this manner is very large. I have no reluctance, in principle, to admit that that may be so. It does, however, seem to me to be quite impossible to believe that, in an advanced economy, the whole of the money stock could be so absorbed. Some part, even if it is quantitatively a small part, must be attributed to voluntary holding; and this voluntary part, whatever its size, is tremendously important. For it is through the voluntary part that monetary disturbances operate, and it is on the voluntary part that monetary policy must have its effect.

This is what I have come to believe about 'Transactions Demand'. I think that Keynes was absolutely right in the distinction which he drew between M_1 and M_2; more exactly right than some of his followers (including myself) have been, when we have formulated the 'Demand for Money' in ways that blurred the distinction. But I rather doubt that he described the distinction in quite the right way. The important thing about M_2 is that it *is* a voluntary demand for money; because it is voluntary it responds to incentive. The important thing about M_1 is that it is not voluntary, save in a very indirect manner. It is the indirect consequence of

[1] R. T. Selden, in M. Friedman, *Studies in the Quantity Theory of Money*; Friedman and Schwartz, *Monetary History of the United States.*

decisions taken for quite other reasons, with no direct cal-culation of their monetary repercussions. It is not a *demand for money*, in the way that the other is. There is no 'Trans-actions Motive' behind it. It is the money that is needed to *circulate* a certain volume of goods, at a particular level of prices. The old Fisher $MV = PT$ gives a better *picture* of it than the over-voluntarized 'Cambridge Quantity Equa-tion'. In relation to this part of the money stock, 'Velocity of Circulation' is perfectly appropriate.

I do not, however, mean that the 'voluntarizing', which came in with Marshall and Pigou and Hawtrey and the early Robertson—long before the *General Theory*—was not, in itself, a step in advance. For there is a voluntary demand for money, and it is this which is the live and exciting part of the monetary problem. (Odd that it was the passive part which they described as 'active' and the sensitive part which they described as 'idle balances'!) All I am saying is that (as so often happens) they took their revolution further than it needed to go. Because they so rightly perceived that there is some voluntary demand, they tried to match the whole stock with that voluntary demand, and so to interpret the whole requirement for money in voluntarist terms. This, I now feel, was confusing; it has sent many of us (myself included) chasing what I now feel to be will-o'-the-wisps.[1]

[1] Among my own works, the latter part of my 'Simplification' article (below, pp. 76–81) is liable to this stricture; so is much of the monetary section of *Value and Capital*. The chief current representatives of the 'over-voluntarizing', which I am here attacking, are, of course, Friedman and Patinkin.

Friedman's interpretation of the statistical tendency towards an in-crease over time in the M/Y ratio (or fall in the income-velocity of circu-lation) that is disclosed by his American figures, as being analogous to the increase in the proportion of income spent on luxuries which follows from a rise in income, does not even at first sight seem very compelling; the analogy does not appear to be close. To seek for an explanation in terms of changes in monetary practices and in monetary institutions, which is the recommendation which would follow from our present approach, looks like being more constructive.

For the 'real balance effect' of Patinkin, see below, p. 52.

THE TWO TRIADS · LECTURE II

Money as store of value

THE point has now been reached when we must switch over
to the 'store of value' function, with the Precautionary and
Speculative Motives which (as has already appeared) are
associated with it. There is no doubt at all that these are
properly described as motives, motives for holding money.
Here, at this end, the notion of a voluntary demand for money
is unquestionably appropriate. These are motives for demanding money to hold, money as a store of value; to a money
which was incapable of being stored, neither could apply.

This voluntary demand for money has been treated by
economists, ever since Keynes, in terms of 'balance-sheet
equilibrium'; and that is the way I shall be treating it in the
present lecture. The approach is conventional, but I believe
that when it is set in its present context we can find some
new things to say about it.

It is curious, at the start, to notice that this 'store of
value' function is much less of a monetary function than the
others we have been examining. A money that could not be
stored might still be used as a unit of account; it might
still be used as a means of payment;[1] if it had these other
functions (even if it had only one of these other functions)
it might still be reckoned as a money of a sort, even if no
more than a *partial money*. But a thing which did not have
these other functions, though it was capable of being carried forward, and maintaining its value (at least to some
extent) on being carried forward, would not naturally be
thought of as being a money at all. Any marketable asset

---

[1] Like the cigarette currency in immediate post-war Germany.

C

which appears on a balance-sheet may be regarded as a store of value; but it does not thereby take on a monetary quality. An insurance policy, even a motor-car, can be a store of value; but it is not money, not even near-money, not even partial money. The other functions, taken by themselves, do confer some monetary quality; the mere capacity of being a store of value does not.

What is it that distinguishes money, regarded as a store of value, from these other assets, which are not money? A pre-Keynesian economist, confronted with this question, would surely have given the obvious answer. Since the mere capacity of acting as a store of value does not confer monetary quality, it must be the other functions which do so. An asset becomes a money asset if it is not only a store of value, but also a unit of account; or not only a store of value, but also a means of payment. If it has these other functions, or even only one of these other functions, and is also storable, it must be reckoned as being money.

This is the obvious answer; and I think I shall be able to show that it is the correct answer. But (since Keynes) it has had a rival. It is commonly said that the essential characteristic of money (regarded as an item in a balance-sheet) is that it does not bear interest, whereas other assets, in some sense or other, do. Thus we are told by Patinkin[1] that what has to be explained is the 'peaceable co-existence' between non-interest-bearing money and interest-bearing bonds. I have myself taken this view in earlier writings,[2] but I have come to hold that it should not be accepted.

I think I shall be able to show, as we go on, that the whole theory makes better sense if we abandon it; but before I come to that, it will be well to observe that there are good practical arguments against it. It has been shown by experience that it is perfectly possible to use a medium of exchange that does bear interest (such as the bill which was used as means of payment in Industrial Revolution Lanca-

[1] *Money, Interest and Prices*, 2nd edition, p. 110.
[2] As on p. 66 below.

shire). It even becomes a question, once one has got that far, whether we do not (more than we realize) do so our-selves. The apparent absence of interest on current accounts in banks is surely to be regarded as a consequence of banking oligopoly; I say 'apparent' for the free provision of services to the depositor of more than a minimum amount is surely to be regarded by the economist as a kind of interest. The thinning and thickening of the line between 'interest-bearing' and 'non-interest-bearing' accounts is easily intelligible in terms of monopolistic (or oligopolistic) discrimination. All these things fit into place, once we abandon the view that 'money' is inherently non-interest-bearing. It may be non-interest-bearing, but it may not.

These, however, are not my basic reasons for wanting to go back to the more traditional view about the nature of money as store of value. I am more influenced by considera-tions which emerge as soon as we try to spell out the balance-sheet theory at all fully. This was not done by Keynes; it has been done more recently, in mathematical terms, by Tobin, Lintner, and several others.[1] I believe that I have found a way in which the essential points can be more simply ex-pressed.

The Theory of Portfolio Selection—the Marginal Advantage curve

Consider (in the first place) the choice before an investor (who may be visualized as the manager of an investment trust) who is concerned to find the best way of dividing a given capital among a number of securities. His object is to get the best result, in terms of yield and risk, *over his whole portfolio*. We begin by supposing that he is just looking for-ward for a limited period (to his next decision-date, we will

    [1] J. Tobin, 'Liquidity Preference as Behaviour towards Risk' (*Review of Economic Studies*, 1958), 'The Theory of Portfolio Selection' (in IEA, *Theory of Interest Rates*, Macmillan 1965); J. Lintner, 'Valuation of Risk Assets and Selection of Risky Investments' (*Review of Economics and Statistics*, February 1965), Hicks, 'Liquidity' (*Economic Journal*, December 1962). Bierwag and Grove, 'Indifference Curves in Asset analysis', *Economic Journal*, June 1966).

say). He should thus (as Keynes, if necessary, will remind him) not only take account of the interest that is offered on each security, but also of the prospect of capital gain or loss; call the two together the *resultant yield*. Each security has a prospect—normally an uncertain prospect—of resultant yield, which may be reduced to formal statement by the following device.

We suppose that the chooser can distinguish a set of alternative *eventualities*, any of which may occur. Which will occur is not known, but the resultant yield on each security, in each eventuality, is supposed to be known. There is thus a matrix of yields, one for each security in each eventuality. This matrix schema (derived, of course, from the Theory of Games) is no doubt a simplification of the problem of choice under uncertainty; but I believe that it retains what are here the essential elements.

Which eventuality will occur is not known, but the probability of its occurrence is supposed to be known. (These, admittedly, are subjective probabilities; they can have no existence except in the mind of the chooser; but that people do have some idea of the 'seriousness' of possible eventualities, and that this is one of the things which influence choice under uncertainty, cannot reasonably be doubted.[1] Then, for each security, its yield in each eventuality (shown on the matrix) together with the probabilities of the eventualities, define the *prospect of that security*.

The *total prospect* for the whole portfolio depends upon these prospects of the individual securities, and upon the proportions in which the capital is divided among the securities. Suppose that the individual security prospects are given. There will then be a total prospect that corresponds to each possible set of proportions in which the capital may be divided. The problem is to choose that set of proportions which gives the 'best' total prospect.

[1] A further refinement of the argument would allow that the probabilities may themselves be uncertain (as argued by W. Fellner, *Probability and Profit*, 1965); but I shall not require that here.

One can, with care, apply something like the usual marginal analysis. An additional pound invested in the jth security will bring about a *marginal advantage* (a marginal *expected* advantage) which measures the gain (say, for the moment, the gain in 'utility') that that additional investment offers, in respect of the whole portfolio. If the portfolio is to be spread over several securities (in an optimum position) the marginal advantage from each security that is used must be equal. If only some of the available securities are selected, the marginal advantage that would be got from investing even a small amount in any of the rejected securities must be less than the (equalized) marginal advantage from the securities that are chosen.

If such spreading is to occur, there must be a 'law of diminishing marginal advantage' corresponding to diminishing marginal utility. For if the marginal advantage (from each security) was independent of the amount invested—if the marginal advantage 'curves' were horizontal—an optimum position would clearly be reached if the whole of the capital were put into that security for which the marginal advantage was highest.

This, which is not an important case in consumer theory, is an important case in the theory of portfolio investment. For it is in these terms that we should treat the case of an investor with no risk-aversion. Such an investor may be defined as one who looks only at the probable yield (strictly, the mathematical expectation of yield) on his whole portfolio. This is simply a weighted average of the probable yields (in the same sense) on the individual securities—an average that is weighted by the proportions of his capital that he puts into them. Thus the marginal advantage, on this test, of investment in the individual security is simply the probable yield on that security; and this (for an investor whose decisions are not big enough to affect prices) is independent of the amount he puts in to that security. Thus, for this type of behaviour (an interesting, though not a very responsible, type of behaviour) the marginal advantage curves will be horizontal lines; so the whole capital will be put into that security for which the probable yield is highest.

As soon, however, as we introduce risk-aversion the position is different; it is then the general case that the curves will be downward-sloping. In order to get this effect, we do (it is true) have to take care to construct the curves in the same way as we have done in the 'no-risk-aversion' case. Just as the curve for any security was there shown as a horizontal line, because risk was not attended to; so in the case of risk-aversion we must show the curve for a security of *certain yield* as a horizontal line, since for such a security it is the same whether risk-aversion does or does not exist. We can do this if we adopt the principle of measuring marginal advantage, not in terms of some subjective 'utility', but in terms of *certainty-equivalent*. That is to say, the marginal advantage got by investing £1 in the *j*th security must be defined as the yield which, if it were certainly expected, would offer the same gain in utility. (It will be noticed, from my choice of this formulation, that I am still an unrepentant ordinalist. Even in this field of risk-theory, where there has been such a come-back of cardinalism, I still prefer—because I find it more convenient—to work in an ordinalist manner.[1]) On this interpretation, the downward slope of the marginal advantage curve can be demonstrated mathematically,[2] at least if we are prepared to accept that the variance, or the standard deviation, of the prospect (which on our assumptions can be defined) is a fair representation of the 'risk' involved in it. But I do not think that we need this mathematical representation as anything more than a general guide. It should be true, much more generally, that successive increments of investment in a risky security (investment in other securities being given) will give a diminishing marginal advantage to an investor with risk-aversion. The practice of

[1] I fully accept the demonstration (by Samuelson and others—*Econometrica*, 1951) that in risk theory, including the Theory of Games, the use of cardinal utility is permissible. But because we may use it, it does not follow that we have to use it.

[2] See below p. 111.

spreading risks is indeed enough (as we have seen) to ensure that this must be the case.

There is, however, a complication at this point, which I must deal with briefly, since it forces itself upon one's attention, though I do not think it affects the main issue with which I am concerned. What happens if there is a correlation (positive or negative) between the prospects of the various securities—if eventualities that are particularly favourable to one are particularly favourable to another—or vice versa? I do not think that this possibility invalidates the marginal approach to portfolio selection, any more than the inter-relatedness of demands (complements and substitutes) invalidates the marginal theory of consumer's behaviour. The chief difference which it makes is the following.

If there is no intercorrelation—if the prospects of the available securities are *independent*—the marginal advantage curve for the individual investment will start, on the vertical axis, at a level which represents the mathematical expectation of yield on that investment. For the marginal advantage (in terms of certainty-equivalent) is always equal to the mathematical expectation of yield *minus* an allowance for the additional uncertainty (over the whole portfolio) which results from the investment of the marginal unit. But if the previous investment in this particular security has been zero—if the marginal unit is a *first* marginal unit, this additional uncertainty (as is evident if we measure it by a quadratic measure such as variance, but the same must presumably hold for other possible measures) is a quantity of the second order of smalls. It follows that whatever is the degree of risk-aversion, the curve will start at the 'probable yield' (or mathematical expectation of yield) and fall to the right from that point.[1]

When intercorrelation is present, this is not so. It will still be true that the 'curve' will fall from left to right, but it will not be true that the initial height is simply a matter of the 'probable yield'. If the new security is positively correlated

[1] Again p. 111.

with some of the other securities which are being used, its introduction will (even initially) increase the variance; so the initial marginal advantage will be less than the 'probable yield'. If it is negatively correlated, the reverse will be the case. And (of course) as soon as we admit intercorrelation, the whole position of the curve will be intimately influenced by the amounts that are to be invested in other securities; but this is the same difficulty as arises from inter-relatedness in consumer theory. It can be dealt with in just the same way.

Now, having got our apparatus, let us use it. It is at once apparent that there is a difference between the case in which there is one investment, out of all those that are available, which has a yield that is *certain*, and the case in which all investments are uncertain. For consider (it is sufficient to establish the point) the uncorrelated case. Even to an investor with risk-aversion the marginal advantage curve for the certain investment (since it is measured in terms of certainty-equivalent) will be a horizontal straight line (at the level of its yield). If this certain investment is used *as well as* some uncertain investments, the marginal advantages of the uncertain investments must be brought down to the same level. The situation is that which is shown in Fig. 1. OK is the amount of capital to be invested; CC' is the (horizontal) marginal advantage curve of the certain investment; UA is the marginal advantage curve of the uncertain investment (supposed for the moment to be the only one). Then CA is put into the uncertain, and AC' into the certain investment. If a second uncertain investment becomes available, we may conveniently draw its marginal advantage curve starting from an axis through K, so that it will appear on the diagram as $U'B$ (Fig. 2). There are then two possibilities, according as B lies to the right of A, or to the left. In the former case an amount AB of the certain investment is still taken, while CA is taken of one uncertain investment, BC' of the other. In the latter case (Fig. 3) the certain investment drops out; ON is put into one of the uncertain investments, NK into the other.

The conclusion is observed to be that the shape of the marginal advantage curve (which here is drawn) represents the increase in movement, that is, the line drawn to the investigating stock of the profit between ... that ... the rate of disadvantage. And it ... . over earlier marginal advantage curve is the same ... and at a certain point it will be indicated. The difference is that it measures ... the ... . The latter measure is ... that and the answer to whether it is an ... which is being made ... which is projected to the ... . the measure to ...

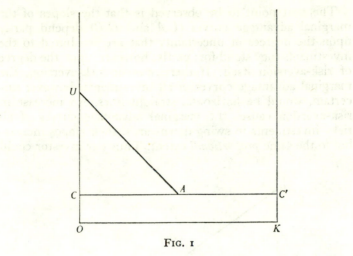

Fig. 1

Now from the marginal advantage curve ... that ... it will be the ... and ... . the latter ... . the information along our ... . that it ... ... and ... . the ... it ... . the ... this ... as ... . and to that ... . On ... it ... that ... . On the other hand ... that ... the ... measure the ... it ... a ... ... which it ... . the latter ... that the ... is ... . that it ... it ... measure the ... to ... .

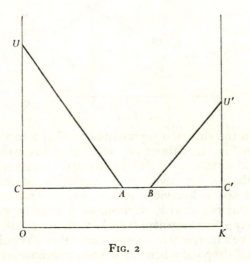

Fig. 2

The next point to be observed is that the slopes of the marginal advantage curves (*UA* and *U'B*) depend partly upon the degrees of uncertainty that are attributed to the investments they stand for; partly, however, upon the degree of risk-aversion itself. If there was no risk-aversion, the marginal advantage curves of all investments, however uncertain, would be horizontal straight lines. An increase in risk-aversion causes the marginal advantage curves of all risky investments to swing downwards, their slopes increasing to the same *proportional* extent. Thus our investor could

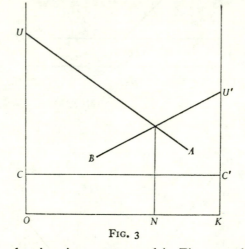

FIG. 3

pass from the situation represented in Fig. 2 to that represented in Fig. 3, without any change in his estimation of prospects, simply by a fall in his risk-aversion. Further, just as the certain investment (inevitably, at least under independence, a low-yielding investment) drops out when there is this fall in risk-aversion, so it may happen that a moderately safe investment (which, with given risk-aversion, would have a marginal advantage curve that was only slightly falling) will drop out when risk-aversion declines still further.

So far, I think it will be agreed, this makes good sense.

The Portfolio theory and the Speculative Motive

But now, in all this, what about Liquidity Preference? I have been careful, in all this formal analysis, not to talk about Liquidity Preference. Yet it is clear that much of what Keynes says about Liquidity Preference—in particular, what he says about the Speculative Motive—will fit in quite well with what we have been doing. Our analysis has proceeded in terms of *resultant yields*, yields that include an allowance for capital gain or loss. Keynes's 'money' can therefore be included among the securities, between which our investor is selecting. Its marginal advantage curve will lie along the horizontal axis; but if no *certain* investment with a higher resultant yield than zero is available, there is no reason why (with sufficient risk-aversion) a positive amount of this 'money' should not be held.

So it is the Keynesian theory of the Speculative Motive which we have been representing (and generalizing). But when it is put in this way, there are several points about it which need comment.

(1) The first is that which I mentioned previously. It is apparent in a new way, on this analysis, that the crucial distinction is not the distinction between a bond that bears interest and a money that does not. The crucial characteristic of money (as it appears in this portfolio theory) is that its resultant yield is certain. If there existed an asset with a positive certain yield, choice between that asset and other assets (of uncertain yields) would proceed upon exactly the same principle. Such an asset, from the point of view of the Speculative Motive, would 'behave like money'. The portfolio would be divided between this asset and other assets in exactly the same way as in the other case. There is thus no reason, so long as we are solely concerned with the Speculative Motive, why savings deposits and such like, which have a certain value at the 'next decision-point', should not reckon as money, even if they bear interest.

(2) The second question is the question of what is meant by *certainty*. The certainty of the yield on money (whether

zero or not) is no more than a certainty in terms of money itself. Why should that signify? If can only signify because money is accepted as 'measure of value' (and so we come back to that other function) or in so far as it is accepted. The Speculative Motive does not only belong to money as 'store of value'; it arises out of the other function, for which Wicksell's expression 'measure of value' is evidently here appropriate; it arises out of this other function also.

Money is only a 'measure of value' if there is some confidence (some minimal confidence) in price-stability—stability, at least in the short run, of those prices with which the investor is chiefly concerned. Here, however, there is a distinction which needs to be made. A general expectation of inflation could be represented on our diagram as a rise in the marginal advantage curves of investments in equities (they shift bodily upwards, it should be noted, not necessarily changing in slope). That in itself is sufficient to diminish the incentive to hold money for the Speculative Motive. Exactly the same change might, however, have been represented (or so it might appear at first sight) if we had decided to work in real terms, so that we reckoned the yield on money as becoming negative. We should get the same diminished incentive to hold money from a downward shift of CC' (below the horizontal axis) as from an upward shift of UA or $U'B$. But this representation would only be valid if the degree of expected inflation were certain; and (in general) it is not. If we are to work in real terms (deflating, let us say, by some index of the prices, of consumer goods or of materials, that are important to the investor), then the yield on money, in those terms, is not just negative; it is also uncertain. Once the investor begins to think in that way, the money has begun to lose its quality as a money asset. (It may still retain its function as a means of payment, as we shall see later.) Once he starts to think in that way, he will be beginning to look about for some new money asset—a foreign money, perhaps—with which to satisfy his requirement for a certain element in his portfolio.

(3) Everything then, so far, fits in; or can be made to fit in. But there is another consequence, which appears to follow from the portfolio theory, and which is more upsetting. Let us look back at Fig. 2. Let us agree that the money which is held (along AB) is held for Keynes's Speculative Motive. But what of the rest of the portfolio? The proportions in which these other securities are held (so far as we can see at present) are determined by the desirability of minimizing total uncertainty over all of them together. That is why (in the case of no intercorrelation) all securities will be used that have a probable yield that is greater than the yield on money (so that their marginal advantage curves start above CC'); all of them must be used so long as any money is held. They will be used, at least to some extent, since total uncertainty can always be reduced by more spreading of risks. The risky securities will be taken in such proportions as will minimize the resultant uncertainty. Beyond that, we can (so far) make no distinction between them.

Put the matter this way. If our investor were content with a yield on his whole portfolio no greater than the yield on 'money', the safest way to get that yield would be to put his whole capital into money. If he desired to do a bit better than that, and was willing to take a small risk in doing so, he should put some of his capital into uncertain assets; but he should not just take a few of the less uncertain assets. He should, in principle, spread the 'speculative' part of his portfolio widely, combining uncertain assets (in theory, *all* of the uncertain assets that have a probable yield that is greater than the yield on money—at least in the 'independence' case) in such a way as to get a bundle that is combined in such proportions as will minimize the resultant uncertainty. Spreading of risks is the great way of diminishing uncertainty. If he becomes a little more ambitious than that, willing to stand a rather greater risk for a higher expectation of yield, the safest way of attaining it is to put less into 'money' and more into the 'bundle', still combining the bundle itself in the same proportions. If his ambition increases further (or his risk-aversion diminishes further—but still subject to the same principle of not taking *unecessary* risk) the proportion of his capital held in money will further diminish, ultimately disappearing. All this while the uncertain securities are combined in proportions that are fixed by the same principle. Only when his demand for 'money' has vanished will there be a change. For if, beyond that point, he still requires a better prospect (in terms of mathematical expectation of yield) he can only get it by rejecting some of the safer (and lower yielding) securities from the bundle, just as money was rejected previously. He should, however, continue to combine those securities which are left in such a way as to minimize uncertainty, spreading his capital widely over such securities as remain.

This is the behaviour which is implied by the Portfolio theory; but how does it square with Liquidity Preference?

There are in fact two versions of Liquidity Preference theory. There is one, which appears to be the version favoured by Keynes[1] in the *General Theory*, in which Liquidity Preference is simply a matter of the demand for money *vis-à-vis* bonds—bonds apparently standing for a bundle of securities in general. There is another, which has some recognition from Keynes in the *Treatise*[2] and which was formally set out in 1935 in my *Suggestion for Simplifying the Theory of Money*; according to this version Liquidity Preference is a matter of the 'spectrum' of assets, assets which may be *more or less* liquid. I think that many economists have assumed that the two versions are practically the same[3] and I have thought so myself; but they are not the same. On the latter interpretation, a fall in Liquidity Preference does not merely reduce the demand for money; it leads to a general

[1] *General Theory*, ch. 13.
[2] *Treatise on Money*, vol. ii, p. 67.
[3] This was also, I think, Keynes's own first reaction. When I sent my 'Simplification' to him, he replied on a postcard (26 December 1934): 'Many thanks for the proof of your article. I like it very much. I agree with you that what I now call *Liquidity Preference* is the essential concept for Monetary Theory.' This was the first that I had heard of Liquidity Preference.

'rightward movement' along the spectrum, a general substitution of less liquid for more liquid assets. Now it is the
former interpretation, according to which there is something
special about the demand for money (at least in the sense of
most certain asset) which the portfolio theory, as it has just
been set out, seems to support; the main effect of a change
in risk-aversion (as I was careful to call it), so long as any
money was being held, was simply a substitution between
money and the 'bundle' of other securities. There was no
room for more liquid and less liquid securities to come into
the movement in different ways, so that there could be a
substitution of one against the other. In this respect the portfolio theory leaves one dissatisfied. There must be something in the other interpretation, which accords so well with
practical experience (banking experience, for example). There
is something here that remains to be cleared up.

Liquidity and the Spectrum of Assets

I begin with one obvious qualification, which one almost
takes as read when one is setting out the portfolio theory,
but which turns out to be worthy of much more serious attention. A practical investor, even if he is operating more or less
according to the principle which I have been describing,
does not in fact spread his 'bundle' over the whole gamut of
securities with positive probable yield, as the theory would
seem to have instructed him to do, or indeed over anything
like the whole gamut. The reason why he does not do so is
clear; it is simply the cost of making transactions, which
economists so easily leave out, but which (as we previously
discovered when we were discussing the Walras system) it is
fatal to leave out when one's subject is money.

Obviously it is transaction cost which limits 'spread'; but
it does much more than that. It introduces another qualification which transforms the whole theory.

If the cost of making transactions were in fact zero, it would
be sufficient to attend, as we have been attending, to the
value of the capital to be invested (*OK* on our diagrams)

without attending to the form in which the capital was initially held. It would be just the same if the capital were initially invested in securities and had to be disinvested, as if it were initially held in money form. That is one point, but there is also another. If transaction cost were zero, it would in fact only be necessary for the investor to look ahead to the 'next decision-point', as we have been supposing him to do. For it would make no difference if he in fact disinvested out of securities at that next decision-point, or did not. He could behave, all the time, as if there were only one investment period of which he needed to take account. He could proceed *as if* he intended to go into cash at the end of the period, so that it would only be the values at which he could expect to perform this realization to which he would have to attend.[1]

Let us take these two points separately, beginning with the second. Let us therefore begin by supposing that he starts with the whole of his initial capital in money form. If he is in fact only looking forward for a single period, intending to realize at the end of that period, no essential difference is made to the preceding theory of his behaviour when we allow for investment costs. The resultant yields from investing in securities, allowance being made for costs of investment *and* disinvestment, are, of course, much lower than they appeared to be when we forgot about those costs. It is perfectly intelligible that in view of those low yields, he will decide to keep the whole of his capital in money form throughout the period. We may then be tempted to say that the money is held *because* of the costs of investment; but the former theory has not in fact ceased to apply.

Now suppose that he is looking further ahead. First of all, instead of planning to realize his whole capital at the end of week 1, let him be planning to realize it at the end of week 2. At the end of week 1, however, he will have an opportunity of changing his policy. If there were no transaction costs, he

[1] His behaviour would then be exactly that which was analysed in the portfolio theory, as it was set out above, and as it is set out in more detail on pp. 103–25 below.

should still behave as he did when he was only looking forward for one week. The best course would be to invest in
the best possible way for week 1 only; then to realize; and
then to invest in the best possible way, on the basis of the
information available at the end of week 1, for week 2. But if
there are transaction costs, this will not do.

If he follows the policy of treating the two weeks separately, he will be involved in transaction costs (of investment
and disinvestment) in each of the two weeks; but if he is
willing to keep to the same pattern of investment over the
two weeks, he will only be involved in one set of transaction
costs. It may well be the case that some investment in securities, which would not be advantageous if the two sets of
transaction costs were to be incurred, will appear advantageous if only one set is to be incurred. But in order to
secure this advantage, he has to deny himself the opportunity of changing his mind. He has to *plan* to limit his own
freedom of action. He has (shall we dare to say it?) to take
up a less *liquid* position.

The further ahead is the date of planned realization, the
stronger is the case for this more adventurous policy. The
stronger will be the case for investment in securities, and
the weaker the case for holding money.

That, however, is not all. To complete the analysis, we
must allow for the fact (it surely is, almost always, a fact)
that in a practical case the planned date of realization is itself
uncertain. This is awkward, but essential; our former device for dealing with uncertainty does, however, still give us
a means of dealing with it. Of the 'eventualities', which
comprise the uncertain element in the prospect, some (we
should now say) are distinguished by differences in the time
that is to elapse before the realization. We can thus (as the
mathematicians would say) partition our matrix, dividing
it into one set of columns which give yields on holding for
one week, one set which gives yields on two weeks, and so on.
(It looks tiresome that the yields are for different periods,
but reflection will show that this does not matter.) The

yields in corresponding columns of the different sets will not be related by a compound interest rule, because of the costs of transactions.

Since, by this device, the problem of portfolio investment (allowing for transaction costs) has been reduced to the same form as that to which we are accustomed, the same (formal) results will emerge. It will still be true that a change in risk-aversion will work in the same way as that which we previously calculated. But there is something very like a change in risk-aversion which will work differently.

An increase in the probability of eventualities, which are such that the date of realization can be shifted into the further future, will increase the probable yield of investment in securities—when allowance is made for transaction cost. An increase in the probability (in the same sense) of require-ment in the near future will increase the demand for money. A demand for money that springs from this cause, I think we shall agree, is precisely what Keynes meant by the Pre-cautionary Motive.

So we have found the Precautionary Motive; but when we have identified it in this way, there is more to it than appears at first. For let us now turn to the other question: of the effect on this decision-taking of the fact that an investor will not usually start with the whole of his capital in money form, but with part of it already invested.

Go back to the case in which he is intending to realize after the first 'week'. So far as the part that is initially held in money form is concerned, the previous argument applies; the resultant yield on investing it for so short a period will be likely to be very low, so that the marginal advantage from investing it will be very low. But if we look at that part which is already invested, the significant choice (in that case) is be-tween realizing it now, or leaving it where it is until the end of the week and then realizing it. There is (effectively) the same transaction cost to be borne in each case; the marginal advantage in leaving it where it is is accordingly unaffected (or nearly unaffected) by transaction cost. It may indeed still happen that the marginal advantage of holding the investment is less than the marginal advantage of holding money, so that some (or all) of a security initially held will be sold out; on that side our former argument applies. Up to the point of the initial holding, the marginal advantage curve is not written down for transaction cost; beyond that point it is. There is thus a *kink* in the curve, just like the kink in the Hall–Hitch theory of oligopoly. For any security not initially held, the curve is (of course) written down for transaction cost from the very start.

Effectively the same thing holds when the date of realization is uncertain. The marginal advantage from investing what was initially money, if there is no confidence that it can remain invested for more than a short time, will be low; but the marginal advantage from maintaining an investment that has already been made will be higher. In this sense, therefore, there will always be a kink.

It is, however, of the greatest importance that the kinks on investments of different sorts will be very different. This is because the costs of disinvestment in securities of different sorts are very different. This is partly a matter of maturity (bills versus bonds), partly a matter of marketability in a wider sense. There are some assets (more liquid assets) which have small kinks, some (less liquid assets) which have bigger ones. That is why there is a *spectrum of assets*—assets which differ from one another in *liquidity*.

The concept of liquidity which we have thus squeezed out is wider than that which was used by Keynes in the *General Theory*. In the *General Theory*, money (according to some definition of money) is *the* liquid asset; all other assets are non-liquid. But in the *Treatise* Keynes had said that one asset is 'more liquid' than another if it is 'more certainly realisable at short notice without loss'.[1] This is a different concept, a relative concept; it is this relative concept of liquidity which we have been analysing here.

One can see that Keynes, during those critical years when

[1] See passage cited on p. 30 above.

he was doing his greatest work, shifted over from the one concept to the other.[1] The reason why he did so is evident; it was done in the interest of simplification. But surely in this instance he over-simplified. The *Treatise* sense of liquidity is an important sense, with which we cannot altogether dispense. It must be brought back into circulation; but it must be sharply distinguished from the other meaning.

I propose, in my next lecture, to mark the distinction in the following way. When I want to refer to money (and close money substitutes) as being liquid assets in the *General Theory* sense, I shall call them *fully liquid*. When I want to refer to assets that have some degree of liquidity, though they are less liquid than money, I shall speak of them as *more or less liquid*. It will not do to describe them simply as less liquid, or semi-liquid, since one must also distinguish them from assets which have no degree of liquidity, being quite unsellable without notice, or having no prospect of being sellable without notice in any probable emergency. The distinction between *more or less liquid* and quite illiquid is also a distinction that we need to retain.

Liquid assets (even those that are only more or less liquid assets) can serve, in a way that quite illiquid assets cannot, as stores of value. Money is in the liquidity spectrum because it is a liquid asset—because it is a store of value. Money is a fully liquid asset, not because of the absence of interest on it, but because of the absence of kink. And that arises out of the other function of money—its function as a means of payment. Although there are transaction costs in switching from one security into money and thence into another security, they are less than those which would be involved if it were sought to barter one security for another directly. (If another intermediary were to be invented which usurped this place of the conventional money, it would also take over the place of fully liquid asset.)

---

[1] In the *Treatise*, liquidity (like some other concepts) is used very loosely. But just because it is used so loosely, it has nuances which escape in the later, more formalized version.

So, in the end, it all seems to tie up. Both the Speculative Motive and the Precautionary Motive are demands for
money to hold: demands for money as a store of value. There
is a Speculative Demand (under suitable conditions of risk-
aversion) because the money that is held is also a 'measure of
value'. There is a Precautionary Demand (which seems now
to be identified as being *par excellence* the Liquidity Demand)
because the money that is held can be used, when required,
as a means of payment. The transactions requirement (as I
preferred to call it) arises out of the functions of means of
payment and measure of value; but it is not a demand for
money *to hold*. So interpreted, the two Triads do, after all,
fit together.

Nevertheless the relation between the Speculative Demand
and the Precautionary Demand seems to have come out a bit
different from the way it is in Keynes. There is something
which still needs to be explained. I shall try, in the concluding
lecture of this series, to look at them again from another
angle.

THE TWO TRIADS · LECTURE III

A classification of assets in general

I BEGIN by observing that we get a new impression of the
Keynesian Triad if we regard it, not simply as a classification of money balances, but as a classification of assets in
general. It can be applied to real assets, and to all sorts of
financial assets, as well as to money. When it is looked at in
this wider way, there are things about it which fit into place,
as they did not quite fit before.

Let us start from the real end, and consider first of all the
real assets of a manufacturing business. They are classified in
familiar ways by the accountant; but though the classification
which I have in mind is related to the accountant's classification, it is by no means the same. The Keynesian classification is a classification by function, or by purpose. There
is, of course, a broad sense in which all its assets are held for
the purpose of making profits; but when we look a little
closer, there are these distinct functions that can be identified.

There are in the first place assets which are required for
the current running of the business—for the production and
for the sale of the firm's output at the rate at which it is running at the moment. If it were not for the danger of confusion
with the wider sense in which the term is used by the accountant, we might call them current assets; but the confusion is
easily avoided by calling them *Running Assets*. The simplest
example of a real running asset, in the case of our manufacturing business, is the goods that are in the pipeline, work in
progress.

The second division, in a classification of this sort, must
obviously consist of *Reserve Assets*—assets that are not re-

quired for the current level of output but are held for emergencies that may arise in the future. Among the real assets which will fit into this category are stocks of materials and other 'spares'—capacity that can be called into use in the event of breakdowns, or of unexpected expansions of demand.

The fixed equipment of a business—its buildings, plant, and machinery—is partly a Running Asset, partly a Reserve Asset. If it is used to capacity, it is fully a running asset; but if it used to less than capacity, the surplus capacity is a reserve. There may, however, be a part of the fixed equipment (as the accountant would regard it) which cannot conveniently be brought into either category. Take the case of plant and machinery, designed for some new venture, which is under construction, or on order. It is not geared to current output, nor is it available as a reserve against emergencies; it is solely held for the sake of the profit which it is expected to earn in due course. I do not think there will be any confusion if we describe an asset of that kind as an *Investment Asset*.

The three categories—Running Assets, Reserve Assets, Investment Assets—can thus be distinguished even among the real assets of a manufacturing business; but the classification is surely one that has a wider application. It can be extended to business of other kinds; and there is even no reason why it should not be extended to the case of the private individual, who has running assets such as the cups and saucers that are used every day for breakfast, and reserve assets such as the spare cups and saucers that can be called into use in the event of breakages, or if his children should happen to bring their friends in for tea. The 'business' which he is running is simply the satisfaction of the current wants of himself and his family; his running assets and his reserve assets have their natural relation to it. Invested savings, invested outside that 'business', are, of course, his investment assets.

These latter, however, are normally financial assets; but it is clear that a similar classification must apply to financial assets also. Among the financial assets to which it applies is money; and when it is applied to money there is a clear link-up with the Keynesian triad. But money is not the only financial asset to which it applies.

Any money that is held as a transaction balance, at the moment when the balance-sheet of the business is taken, will reckon as a running asset. If production has a cycle (say a seasonal cycle) there will be a clear ebb and flow between work in progress, stocks of finished product, and this money balance; they must clearly be reckoned together as running assets of the business. Much the same will hold for the weekly cycle of the wage-earner. The amount of money that is held (on the average) in this way will be a consequence of the general pattern of production (or consumption) on which the unit is engaged; it is the money requirement for this current pattern. If sufficient money (from whatever source) is not available to satisfy this requirement, it will be necessary that the activity of the unit should in some way be contracted; but activity cannot in general be expanded just by making more money available as a running asset. Surplus money, like surplus stocks of materials, automatically becomes a reserve asset; thus it is only through its impact upon the 'portfolio' of reserve assets that it can exercise an effect. It was for this reason that I insisted (in my first lecture) that the requirement of money for this 'transaction' purpose should not be regarded as a voluntary *demand* for money.

The only other financial asset which can appear as a running asset is trade credit—representing goods that have been sold but not yet paid for. Trade credit enters in the same way into 'cycle' of production and sale. The expansion of trade credit introduces a lag between the expansion of productive activity (or of the money value of production) and the expansion of the money requirement which it will normally engender. This is a lag which may be very important from the point of view of monetary policy; but for present purposes we may merely note that here is its place, and pass on.

Substitution among Reserve Assets

Apart from trade credit, which is a deferment of payment, a financial asset can appear among the running assets of an ordinary business[1] (or indeed of a private individual) only if it is a means of payment; and therefore, as we have seen, it must *be* money. Money, however, is by no means the only financial asset that can be held as a reserve asset. We shall clearly identify the Precautionary Demand for money with the demand for money as a reserve asset; but it is vital, in this case, that money, to be held as a reserve asset, can be substituted by other forms of holding reserves. There is thus, in this sector, an operation upon a Liquidity Spectrum.

It is essential, if a financial asset is to function as a reserve asset, that it should possess some degree of liquidity. It must, at the least, be 'more or less liquid'. It need not be fully liquid, but it must possess liquidity in that looser *Treatise* sense, of being 'realisable at short notice without loss'; it must, at the least, be readily marketable. Assets which are not readily marketable may serve as reserve assets for some particular purpose (as is the case with the real reserve assets of which I have already given examples); but a financial asset, kept as a reserve asset, is held to be available for use in some as yet unspecified emergency. In order to serve this general purpose, it must be a marketable asset; it must possess at least the weaker sort of liquidity.

From the point of view of liquidity, the financial assets that can be held as reserve assets will usually be rather close substitutes; so it is highly likely that there will be a regular 'Liquidity Preference' substitution between them. In a given state of confidence it will be more tempting to hold reserve assets in less liquid forms the higher is the interest they offer; a shock to confidence will lead to a movement in the direction of greater liquidity. It should, however, be emphasized that the kinds of assets which are *more or less liquid* will change from time to time, with changes in the

[1] There is an important exception in the case of financial businesses, as we shall see later (p. 48 below).

organization of the economy that is under consideration; and even at the same time there will be differences in the kinds of such assets that are available to one operator and to another. Transaction costs will not be the same for one as for another; it is only such as have low transaction costs *for him* that the particular operator can use as his more or less liquid assets. Thus the spectrum of assets which is effectively available will be different for the large firm with good 'city' connexions, on the one hand, and for the small firm or small private capitalist (who is using his savings as a cushion against emergencies) on the other.

It is not only financial assets, in the usual sense, which can be used as more or less liquid reserve assets—being available, that is, for use in as yet non-specified emergencies. Actual stocks of commodities (even raw materials of a durable and fairly homogeneous character) will usually involve the holder in substantial costs of resale, so that they can hardly be regarded even as more or less liquid assets.[1] But claims upon commodities, which have not yet entailed a physical delivery, may well on occasion be more or less liquid. Liquidity preference substitution, among reserve assets, will then carry right over into the markets on which such commodities are traded, so that prices in these markets may be *directly* affected by liquidity shifts.

I have much more to say about reserve assets, but it had better be postponed until we have cleared our minds about the third sector.

Substitution among Investment Assets

If an asset is held as a (general) reserve asset, it must at least be more or less liquid; but if it is held as an investment asset, this is by no means the case. It is by no means the case, even if we insist that an investment asset is an asset that is in some

---

[1] It is curious that Keynes in the *Treatise* (vol. ii, ch. 29), described stocks of commodities as 'liquid capital', without considering whether they are 'more or less liquid' or not. But this is a usage which has not caught on, and it is clear that for precision of thinking it should be avoided.

sense 'outside the business' of its holder. Land and buildings may be held (as for instance by Oxford and Cambridge colleges) strictly as investment assets, though they are very illiquid. An investment asset is held for its yield; and an asset may have a quite satisfactory yield, even though it would be a complicated operation to dispose of it.

One can conceive of a world—and there may well have been a time when it was not a bad model of the real world—in which investment funds would normally be held in forms from which, for the holder, there were high costs of disinvestment; so that it would normally be expected, when an investment was made, that it would continue to be held, if not indefinitely, at least for quite a long period. In such a world investments would be selected according to the yields that were expected from them, without attention to capital appreciation; though there would still be an allowance for uncertainty of yield, for the possibility that the expected yield, over some part of the period of holding, would not be attained. Choice between investments could still proceed, very nearly, according to the principles that were set out in our portfolio selection theory;[1] excepting that since previously made investments could not be undone, it would only be new investments which could be freely selected. These, however, could still be chosen so as to get the best balance between yield and uncertainty of yield, taking account of the given prospects of the old investments. The greater the willingness to bear risks, the more likely it would be that the investor, making his new investment, would go for a high-yielding asset of uncertain yield; the greater his risk-aversion, the more likely it would be that he would go for a 'safe security'.

I think one might say that in a world of this sort, in which investments had to be chosen as long-period investments, there could be no demand for money, or at least for a non-interest-bearing money, as an investment asset. However great the risks of investment in income-yielding securities, a security without yield—when the whole point of the selection was to

[1] pp. 20–26; see also pp. 103–25 below.

get yield—would never be chosen. There might indeed be some money that was waiting to be turned into an investment asset. Some of the savings coming forward at any time (not by any means all of what would be reckoned as savings by the social accountant) would be coming forward initially in money form; and it might well be that those money balances would have to accumulate into minimum amounts before the costs of investing them could be faced. Such savings, on their way to being invested, might be reckoned as embryonic investment assets, or they might be regarded as a particular form of running asset, tied on to the saving process in the same way as other running assets are tied to current production. If we take the latter view (and it seems to me that it is on the whole the more useful view) we can say, quite simply and without qualification, that in this non-speculative economy there will not be any money (certainly no non-interest-bearing money) among investment assets.

Money does not appear among the investment assets because there is no speculation; the demand for money, as an investment asset, is the Speculative Demand. It is, however, most important to emphasize that the reason for the appearance of Speculation is not a change in attitude. There is no speculation in the economy which I have been describing for a reason that is purely objective; there can be no speculation in securities, because the costs of investment and disinvestment are too high. As soon as these costs are reduced, it will pay to speculate—or to 'manage one's portfolio'—simply in order to get the best return on that portfolio; it will pay to do so even if one's only concern is *income*.

If the investor thinks that the price of a security, which he proposes to buy, will be substantially lower in the future than it is now, it will pay him to postpone his purchase. If the security, yielding 6 per cent. on its face value, is now standing at 100, and if he is confident that in six months' time it will be standing at less than 97, he can keep his money idle for the six months, losing six months' interest, but even with that deduction having £97 for every £100 which he would have invested. If his guess is right, he will have a higher income from that point onwards than he would have had if he had taken the other course. He has merely to take the *private* decision to reckon the 3 per cent. which he has deducted as being 'income'. The income which he derives is then at the rate of 6 per cent. per annum for the first six months, and more than 6 per cent. per annum there-after; which, strictly in income terms, is more than he would have got if he had invested to get a flat 6 per cent. per annum throughout. The money which he has held for the Specula-tive Motive has not, when a longer view is taken, been with-out yield.

It is evident that it was through his thinking about bear speculation such as this that Keynes lighted upon the Specu-lative Motive. What is effectively the same thing does indeed appear in the *Treatise* as 'excess-bearishness'. But in the *General Theory* he takes it further. What he is there contem-plating is something which corresponds to the limiting case which I analysed in my second lecture;[1] the case in which costs of investment and disinvestment are negligible, so that the only thing which matters to the rational investor is the value of his portfolio in the near future—capital value including accumulated interest. This will still be so in that limiting case, for the reason just given, even if the ultimate objective is the maximization of yield, over the whole port-folio, in the longer run. Once this point is reached, it becomes possible that a non-interest-bearing money may be held for the Speculative Motive, even though there is no expectation (in the mean value sense) of a fall in the price of securities. It may simply be held because of risk-aversion, because of a desire to diminish the uncertainty of the future value of the portfolio, or of the resultant yield, as I previously called it.[2] Behaviour of this kind is speculative behaviour, though it is not based upon Hope, but on Fear. Money that is held in this way is an Investment Asset, held for the Speculative Motive.

[1] pp. 21–26.   [2] See, however, pp. 116–17 below.

Funds and Financiers

In this interpretation of the Speculative Motive I have, I think, followed Keynes quite closely; but when the matter is set out in this way, it seems to lead to one result which is not in complete conformity with the impression that one gets from Keynes. Keynes, I think, believed that it was always (or nearly always) the case—in an economy with developed financial markets—that there would be *some* money being held for a speculative motive; but in the version given here it does not seem to come out like that.

I have admitted that risk-aversion *may* induce the investor to hold some non-interest-bearing money in his portfolio, even if he is not being bearish about expected mean value; but nothing has been said which would lead us to suppose that he must do so, unless he is feeling in a very poor state. One must indeed grant to Keynes that it takes all sorts to make a market; so that for some to be *relatively* bearish and some *relatively* bullish is perfectly normal. But this does not show that there must be some who are absolutely bearish. It is hard to see why it is necessary that an appreciable number of those operating should have so high a degree of risk-aversion that they will hold non-interest-bearing money for a speculative motive, even when there is no particular reason why the market should go down rather than go up.

The reason which Keynes gives for his view that the speculative demand for money is always positive (in an economy with developed financial markets) is that without the existence of such speculative balances, open-market operations by the Monetary Authority would be impossible.[1] It is only, he thinks, by the absorption of such speculative balances that the Monetary Authority is able to reduce the supply of money to the market by selling securities; reducing the price of the securities (raising the rate of interest) to whatever extent is needed for the necessary absorption to take place. Experience since 1936 may throw some doubt upon

[1] *General Theory*, p. 197.

this alleged 'fact'; have we not heard of new issues that 'had to be taken up by the Departments'? The facts for which we have to account are a little different from those that were before Keynes. But even apart from that, there is more to be said.

Once we appreciate that the rise in the importance of the speculative motive is a consequence of the rise of financial markets (for it is the marketability which they provide which reduces the costs of investment and disinvestment), we ought surely to bring these markets into the picture much more explicitly. It is implied in the existence of financial markets that there exist financial middlemen (just as the existence of middlemen is a necessary condition for the working of any organized market). The kinds of middlemen (or financial intermediaries) who operate upon developed financial markets are legion; we shall not need to distinguish between them. But we cannot complete our picture until these Financiers (as I shall call them for brevity) have been given a place in it in their own right.

They have not, so far, had a place. The investor, whose management of his portfolio of securities we have been laboriously analysing, is not a Financier; he is what, by contrast with the Financier, may be called a Fund. A Fund is a body to which a certain capital has been entrusted, with no obligation but to make the return on that capital as large as possible. In a purely accounting sense, it has liabilities, but its liabilities are 'asleep'. Thus it is solely on the assets side of its balance-sheet that it has to operate. It may pay dividends out of its gains, but they are not contractual liabilities. There are many kinds of Funds: some sorts of Investment Trusts, the investment departments of endowed charities, as well as the investment portfolio of the private capitalist.

A Financier, by contrast, has liabilities that are not asleep. The private speculator, speculating on borrowed money, is an amateur financier, a Fund that is playing at being a Financier. It does not much matter if we follow Keynes and treat him as a Fund, regarding the money balances that he holds (if he holds any) as speculative balances. But surely we can now see that the professional Financier has to be treated differently. He is in business to deal in securities—including marketable securities (bills, bonds, and equities) and more or less unmarketable securities (such as mortgages and bank advances). Many of the same securities as are held by Funds as investment assets are held by Financiers for the direct purpose of their financial business. But this, in terms of our present classification, means that they are not for the Financier investment assets; they are running assets or reserve assets. The character of a financial business is such that a large part of its assets would naturally be regarded as reserve assets. As such, we should expect them to be liable to liquidity shifts—and surely they are! Surely it is in the operation of those who deal professionally upon financial markets that we have the clearest and most obvious appearance of Liquidity Preference!

Does not everything fit into place once we admit that the assets of the professional financier are predominantly *reserve* assets: assets that are held in forms that are largely determined by the need to have them easily convertible into money to deal with emergencies? Emergencies, of course, that may arise on either side. They may be related to the 'volatile' character of a part, at least, of his liabilities; or they may be related to the possible occurrence, at nearly any moment, of new opportunities for doing financial business. *We must then draw the conclusion that the corresponding demand for money is a Precautionary Demand.* We can then say, quite simply and quite generally, that it is the Precautionary Demand for money which is the demand for liquidity. Anyone, whether or not he is a Financier, has a precautionary demand for money, whenever he has a need for liquidity; and the need for liquidity is a need for a means of being covered against emergencies.

If we say this, and it will make things much more straightforward if we are allowed to say it, it will follow that the

Speculative Demand for money is being taken down a peg from the place which it occupies in Keynes. We do not deny that it may exist; but it is a special, not a general phenomenon. We must not make it essential to the working of the Financial System. It should therefore be useful to begin one's analysis of the Financial System with a First Part in which it is left out of account.

One may indeed go rather further. The theory of the working of the Financial System (stripped of all conventions, institutions, and institutional jargon) should probably be divided into three parts, not two. The first, which we may call the Liquidity theory—the Liquidity theory *proper*—will tell the story entirely in terms of financial running assets and financial reserve assets; this can be put in quite a simple form, and for many purposes it is quite good enough. Even in the second part, we should not introduce the speculative demand for money; but we should take account of speculation, in more general terms. This second part is thus a generalization of the theory of short and long interest rates. Only in the third part should we come to the speculative demand for money—the 'Liquidity trap', or the 'Speculative trap', as it would have been better to call it. I shall try to sketch out, in very broad outline, how these three parts should go.

The working of the Financial System—First Part

Consider, in the first place, the effect of a sale of securities by the Monetary Authority. We do not (here) have to specify what securities; but we may assume that they are readily marketable securities, such as could be held, in the balance-sheet of any unit that absorbs them, as financial reserve assets. They could be absorbed, as more or less liquid assets, into the balance-sheet of any holder of reserve assets; but it is likely that they will mostly be absorbed, in the first place, by financiers. It may be that their first lodgement is among the running assets of financiers; but if so they will be passed on. Thus we may take it that they will come to rest among someone's reserve assets. Taking the whole of this first stage together, there has been an exchange, by the successive parties to the transaction taken as a whole, of some money taken from a reserve balance (or precautionary balance) against the securities that have been sold (or issued) by the Monetary Authority.

Someone, therefore, has had to take up a less liquid position, having exchanged the (fully liquid) money for a security which is no more than more or less liquid. In order that such a position should be voluntarily taken up, the price of the security must fall (that is to say, the rate of interest—in some sense—must rise). In view of the substitutability among reserve assets, there must normally be some fall in price which will induce the shift. (But conditions may sometimes occur in which the precautionary balances which are accessible, in the short run, to such substitution are not sufficient to enable a large issue to be taken up immediately; as we find.)

What happens next? Again because of the substitutability between more or less liquid assets, the fall in the price of securities will communicate itself, to some extent or other, to securities other than those which have been issued by the Monetary Authority. And if there are any real assets (such as claims on commodities) which are sufficiently liquid to be held as reserve assets, these also will fall in price—this being a first way in which the contraction may be transmitted to commodity markets. I see no reason why this should not be a real effect, though it will depend upon the organization of the economy in question how important it is. In an economy where organized produce markets have a central position, and in which they are fairly free to operate, much importance could be attached to this 'Hawtrey effect' as it will be natural to call it.[1] That condition may well have been satisfied in nineteenth-century England, and it may have been satisfied, even at a later date, in the United States. But Keynes was surely right in maintaining (in the *Treatise*) that already

---

[1] *Currency and Credit* (1919), *passim*. It is, of course, a general theme throughout Sir Ralph Hawtrey's works.

in the England of the nineteen-twenties the Hawtrey effect was, on the whole, something of a back number.

But that is by no means all. There has been a (more or less) general fall in the prices of securities, especially of such securities as are held as reserve assets. Thus the money values of the portfolios of securities, held by businesses of all kinds as reserve assets, will have fallen. (This applies, it should be emphasized, not only to those who have made the original switch, but to anyone who is holding such securities as reserve assets.) Now the desired money value of reserve assets must bear some relation—even if it is only a rather vague relation—to the money value of turnover; thus if the money value of reserves has fallen, while the money value of turnover has not yet fallen, there are likely to be some businesses, at least, who will be feeling their reserves to be insufficient. If one is starting from a position in which business as a whole has more than sufficient reserves, it will be easy to fill the gap by borrowing from others. But if there is no such general excess of liquidity, the only way in which the gap can be filled is by raiding the firm's running assets, operating in consequence at a lower level of activity. Here we have another way in which pressure on liquidity may escape from the 'financial' into the 'industrial' circulation.[1]

What is indeed at bottom the same process may be more readily recognizable in another form. When business is operating upon credit from a financier (say a bank) it will be the bank which feels the direct pressure upon its reserve assets, and which endeavours to restore its liquidity by contracting the credit on which its clients have come to rely. They then have no alternative but to draw money from their running assets. So stated, the process is very familiar; but this is where it fits in.

There can thus be no question of the importance (or the potential importance) of this 'liquidity pressure' effect on the

---

[1] It should be noted that the 'liquidity pressure' effect is a 'wealth effect' (corresponding to the income effect of *Value and Capital*). The 'Hawtrey effect' is a substitution effect.

side of contraction. But let us see what happens on the other tack.

Up to a point the process will correspond. New money is being issued by the Monetary Authority through the purchase of securities. As before, there will be a first stage at which the new money finds a home among someone's reserve assets, replacing (among those reserves assets) the securities that have been purchased by the Monetary Authority. The seller has had to move in the direction of greater liquidity; in order to induce him to take up this more liquid position—more liquid than he would have chosen at the old price (or rate of interest)—the price of the security will have to rise (the rate of interest to fall). Substitution upon the liquidity spectrum, once again, is sufficient for this shift to come about.

If conditions are such that there can be a 'Hawtrey effect' that is at all significant, this should work on the expansion, just as on the contraction side. I do not think that in that case there need be any asymmetry. But the position is different with respect to the 'liquidity pressure' effect.[1]

There is no doubt at all about the urgency of the compulsion to keep the value of one's reserve assets *at least* at some minimum level. If they fall below that level action must be taken, even if it is the desperate action of raiding one's running balance. But there is no such corresponding compulsion on the other side. If the value of the securities kept as reserve assets rises, so that it becomes larger than the minimum thought to be necessary, there is no obvious necessity for the surplus to be transferred to running assets.[2] There is another place for it, a place which it will automatically occupy if no action is taken—among investment assets. This

[1] This is the fundamental point on which (I think) I still differ from Patinkin. His 'real balance effect' corresponds to my 'liquidity pressure effect' on the side of restriction; but he makes it work both ways, and there I part company.

See his answer to my review of the first edition of his book (*EJ*, 1959) and the corresponding passage in the second edition (pp. 349–54). I fully admit that in my review (*EJ*, 1958) I had not got the point right.

[2] As Patinkin (in effect) supposes it to be.

—simply this—is the basic reason for the asymmetrical effect of monetary management.

It must, of course, be granted that while a process of contraction (in turnover) is occurring, while unwelcome decisions are having to be made in many places under liquidity pressure, a relaxation of the pressure, by enabling these decisions to be avoided, can do a good deal to moderate the decline. But when business has settled down to a low level, the case is surely different. Additional liquidity will make expansion possible; but it is not easy to see that it can be an effective agent for bringing it about.

All of this can be said (it must be emphasized) before we leave what I have called the First Part of the theory. It already comprises what are, perhaps, the most important things. One could go into much more detail about them, even when one was keeping to the plane of generality to which I am confining myself in the present discussion. But enough has probably been said to indicate the lines which further elaboration would follow.[1]

Second Part—the influence of Speculation

So I turn to the Second Part, which may be conveniently (here) approached by a consideration of Keynes's views (in the *General Theory*) about the long-term rate of interest.

He did not believe in the Hawtrey effect, and (no doubt because he was looking for means of expansion) he was not much interested in the liquidity pressure effect; but he still (at least at that time) retained some faith in the influence of

---

[1] One important way in which the analysis of this section is over-simplified is in its neglect of *conditional* contracts—contracts to pay on the occurrence of particular eventualities; or even (to some extent) at the will of the creditor or indeed of the debtor. The conditional assets and liabilities which thus arise need more working in than I have given them. (Insurance contracts, underwriting, bank overdrafts are obvious examples.) It is easy to see how these contracts arise; by using them a given gain in liquidity can be got on easier terms. By attending to them I could have made my analysis sound more realistic, though it would at the same time have been much more complicated. I do not think that it would have greatly changed the general character of the analysis.

the long rate of interest upon industrial investment. He did indeed believe that the changes in the long rate that could be induced by monetary policy were less than might at first be expected—owing to the tendency of speculation (operating through the speculative demand for money) to stabilize the long rate. Even so, he believed that such effect as could occur was of major importance.

Experience since 1936, and especially since the early fifties, has not been very favourable to his conjectures in this field—to either of them. The long rate of interest, even (so far as there is such a thing) the world long rate, has proved remarkably volatile. It has jumped from (say) 3 per cent. to (say) 6 per cent.—from what used to be regarded as very low to what used to be regarded as very high; and the effect upon industrial investment has been hard to distinguish. In order to account for this later experience, we must surely subject the Keynes theses on these matters to a thorough revision.

I shall not attempt that revision here, but shall confine myself to a couple of points.

The pattern of short and long rates that exists in the market at any time depends, broadly speaking, on two factors: (1) on the relation between the relative supplies of securities of various maturities, and (2) upon speculative anticipations of the way in which interest rates, in general, will move in the future. On account of the first factor, it is possible to manipulate the pattern by 'funding and unfunding', by varying the proportions of issues of different maturities that are bought and sold by the Monetary Authority; but there is always the speculative factor that is also in operation. If monetary stringency (or monetary ease) is expected to be short-lived, it will have a significant effect on short rates, but its effects on long rates will be damped down by speculation. This, of course, was the situation that was mainly in Keynes's mind. But it is not the only possibility. He himself, in one of those qualificatory passages which are more abundant in the *Treatise* than in the later work, draws attention to the possibility that a change in Bank Rate (and the same would hold for any other distinguishable action by the Bank) may 'constitute a new fact—by throwing new light, for example, upon the policy and intentions of the currency authority'.[1] When this is allowed for—and in the post-1950 world it has surely very much to be allowed for—the effect of speculation on the interest-rate structure may be very different from what it usually was in the old days. Everything depends on whether the Bank 'looks as if it means business' or if it looks as if it does not. Everything depends upon the atmosphere, even the political atmosphere, in which the action is taken, and upon the degree of resolution which seems to be imputable to the action itself.

That is one thing. The other concerns the effect of interest (the long rate of interest) upon industrial investment, supposing that conditions are such that the long rate can move significantly. This, very soon after the *General Theory* appeared, became a subject for widespread scepticism;[2] and the scepticism has not much diminished since. If we call it the 'Keynes effect', to match the 'Hawtrey effect', it also (the average economist would now say) has become a back number. Perhaps it is a back number; but there is still one thing which I should like to say about it.

I would like to suggest that what Keynes overlooked was the lack of correspondence between *net* investment (in the sense of the accountant—or social accountant) and *new* investment, in a sense which is highly relevant to business decisions. Any piece of real investment alters the 'prospect' before the business (in much the same sense as we have used that word in the theory of Portfolio Selection). It alters it in two ways—by changing the physical equipment and by changing the financial structure (since any additional equipment has somehow to be paid for). The total effect on the prospect (including the uncertainty of the prospect) is partly

[1] *Treatise*, vol. i, p. 202.
[2] Set off, perhaps, by the famous Oxford inquiry (*Oxford Economic Papers*, Nos. 1-3, reprinted in T. Wilson and P. W. S. Andrews, *Oxford Studies in the Price Mechanism*, pp. 1-74).

an effect of the one, partly of the other. On the financial side, there is probably a loss in liquidity, though the loss may be damped down if the finance can be had on convenient terms. But what of the real side? The asset which is being acquired is (usually) itself quite illiquid; but it is the effect of acquiring it on the uncertainty of the prospect before the whole enterprise which is the thing that matters. And this may go either way. We should distinguish between 'defensive investment',[1] which is undertaken to diminish the uncertainty of the prospect before the business, and genuinely *new* investment, which in itself increases uncertainty. As examples of defensive investment, we can include not only much normal replacement, but such things as the provision of facilities needed to retain one's labour force, and the accumulation of stocks of finished product so as to enable orders to be filled with sufficient promptitude to keep one's customers in humour. And the installation of new kinds of equipment, to exploit new techniques of production, though they are new investment from the point of view of the first installer, becomes defensive investment from the point of view of his competitors, who have to follow suit if they are not to be left in a dangerous position by being left behind.

The marginal advantage of defensive investment will usually be high; it will be undertaken, so long as the necessary finance is available, on almost any terms. Quite severe liquidity pressure will have to be applied in order to stop it. New investment, on the other hand, is a much more sensitive creature. Thus it may be that the reason why it is hard to control investment in a boom is that in the boom (so long as it is expected to continue) most investment has become defensive investment; and the reason why it is hard to start up investment in a slump is that it cannot be done without stimulating new investment. And the financial terms which are sufficient by themselves to stimulate new investment, when it has turned sluggish, are hard to offer.

[1] I borrow the term from Lamfalussy (*Investment and Growth in Mature Economics*) though I do not use it quite in his sense.

Third Part—the Trap

That brings us, of course, to the 'Speculative Trap'—now to be looked at again, in the light of what I have more lately been saying. How much—if anything—is left of it?

There are two questions to be considered, and it is essential to distinguish them. There is the 'short-period' question, about the effectiveness of monetary policy in engineering recovery from a slump; and there is the 'long-period' question, of the ability of a financial system (such as usually assumed) to adjust itself to a condition in which the marginal productivity of capital has got 'permanently' stuck at a low level. Keynes himself set the fashion of taking these two questions together. I am nevertheless convinced that to do so is a mistake.

So far as the short-period question is concerned—so far as the difficulty of engineering recovery from depression by monetary means is concerned—there is no conflict between what has been said here and what was said by Keynes. It has been fully accepted, in the course of the preceding argument, that in speculative markets that are smitten by risk-aversion, money may be held idle for a speculative motive; and that the provision of additional money by the monetary authority may do no more (or negligibly little more) than pile additional funds into these idle balances.[1] On all this I have nothing further to add. I would, however, insist that what matters is not the effect on the 'long rate of interest' in the sense of the yield on long-term government bonds; what matters is the terms on which finance is made available to industry, and this is by no means the same thing. The 'financial circulation' may be flooded, and even so the money may fail to get through.

The long-period question, I now hold, is rather different.

[1] An increase in the supply of money, used to finance additional government spending, will, of course, increase activity while it is occurring (through the usual saving-investment mechanism). All that is relevant to the present discussion is the effect on the 'equilibrium' position after the expenditure is over. I see no reason why it should be impossible that the additional money should then be absorbed (as Keynes supposed) into speculative balances.

While one can understand that large balances may be held idle for considerable periods, for a speculative motive, it is harder to grant that they can be so held indefinitely. An investment asset, I have insisted, is (even by the speculator) ultimately held for its yield. The 'trap' can hardly work in the same way in the long period as in the short. There may nevertheless be something that more or less corresponds.

There is a simplified, but still useful, model of the financial system which would represent it as a hierarchy of financiers, who may be arranged in rings. Each ring lend to the ring outside it and borrows from the ring inside it; at the centre of all the rings is the Central Bank. Industry can raise funds at various points of the rings; but in order that its needs should be fully met, each of the rings must play its part. In equilibrium, each of the financiers, wherever situated, has to make a profit and each has his problem of liquidity. He will not raise funds from the ring inside him, and lend funds to the ring outside, unless he gets a net advantage from so doing; and in order to get a net advantage, he must lend at a higher rate than that at which he borrows. Some of the funds that go out to industry must thus (again in equilibrium) bear a total cost which is made up of several of these margins; they will thus be included in the marginal cost of capital to industry. Even if the rate of interest, as it appears at the centre of the system—from the Central Bank to the inner ring—is reduced to zero, or almost to zero, the marginal cost of capital to industry will not be reduced to zero. It is in this sense that there can be a 'floor to the rate of interest' (the effective rate of interest) even in long-period equilibrium.[1]

The floor that is so determined depends, however, upon the assumption of a given financial system. By improvements in organization the costs of getting funds to industry can be reduced; and it is very arguable that in a stagnant economy (where the problem of the 'floor' might become acute) no elaborate organization for this purpose would be required. But some organization would be required; for it is not possible

---

[1] For a fuller discussion, see my *Capital and Growth*, ch. 23.

to think that any economy could be rationally organized in which anyone could borrow funds for nothing, on nothing more than his own statement that he needed them. Some kind of sifting must always be required, and some kind of organization to do the sifting. Any such organization must have costs attached to it.

These are indeed questions which do not now have the urgency that they seemed to have (for a while) in the nineteen-thirties. But the issue of the efficiency of financial organization, to which they draw attention, is a continuing problem. It is not a thing which, even now, we ought to take at all for granted.

Conclusion

We have come a long way from the Two Triads. It is hard to sum up.

What I have tried to present in these lectures is a view of money which shall not only fit in with what we know about non-monetary economics, but shall also be consistent with the broad facts of monetary evolution. Money is not a mechanism; it is a human institution, one of the most remarkable of human institutions. Even the simplest forms of money, even metallic coinage, even the use of metals as money that preceded coinage, none can function without some minimum of trust. As mutual confidence increases (within circles that are first of all narrow, but gradually widen) the forms of money that can be used become more subtle, more economical, but at the same time more fragile. At the earlier and cruder stages, mechanical theories (such as the Quantity Theory) give a reasonably good approximation to the working of money; but the subtlety of the monetary facts has gone on increasing, and theory has had a hard job to keep up.

A fully developed monetary system (as so far experienced) is very sensitive, and is therefore unstable. It was already true, in the nineteenth century,[1] that some people were

[1] See pp. 164–6, 174–88 below.

beginning to recognize the fact of that instability, and were deliberately seeking to develop monetary institutions which should operate, not to increase instability, but to diminish it. So we came to the growth of Central Banks. But Central Banks had two limitations. One (which I have emphasized in these lectures) is that when it is mainly through the 'liquidity pressure' effect that they have to operate, they are better at preventing over-expansion than at preventing over-contraction. The other (which I have not mentioned explicitly, though I am sure it will have been taken for granted in what I have been saying) is their limitation to national economies: that they have been *national* central banks. Only in a national economy that is largely self-contained, can a national central bank be a true central bank; with the development of world markets, and (especially) of world financial markets, national central banks take a step down, becoming single banks in a world-wide system, not at the 'centre' any longer. Thus the problem that was (partially) solved by the institution of national central banks has reappeared, and is still unsolved (though we are trying to solve it), on the world level.

Meanwhile it has been thought that the other defect had been dealt with, by bringing in the government budget as an alternative, or as an additional, stabilizer. That, of course, is the revolutionary idea which emerged from the *General Theory* (though, when one reads the book, it comes out a bit through the back door). I have deliberately kept away from it in these lectures, as it was the other side of Keynes's work (and of other work which has followed from it) on which I hoped to throw some light. There would have been plenty to say on the 'fiscal' side, if one had wished to do so, for the implementation of the 'revolution' is not proving to be such a simple matter. One of the difficulties, it may be noticed, is parallel to that which has arisen on the banking side—that national budgets are the budgets of national governments. They are rather a curious means of controlling a monetary system that has become so international.

4

A SUGGESTION FOR SIMPLIFYING THE THEORY OF MONEY (1935)[1]

I

AFTER the thunderstorms of recent years, it is with peculiar diffidence and even apprehension that one ventures to open one's mouth on the subject of money. In my own case these feelings are particularly intense, because I feel myself to be very much of a novice at the subject. My education has been mostly in the non-monetary parts of economics, and I have come to be interested in money only because I found that I could not keep it out of my non-monetary problems. Yet I am encouraged on reflection to hope that this may not prove a bad approach to the subject: that some things at least which are not very evident on direct inspection may become clearer from a cross-light of this sort.

It is, of course, very largely by such cross-fertilization that economics progresses, and at least one department of non-monetary economics has hardly emerged from a very intimate affair with monetary theory. I do not, however, propose to resume this particular liaison. One understands that most economists have now read Böhm-Bawerk; yet whatever that union has bred, it has not been concord. I should prefer to seek illumination from another point of view—from a branch of economics which is more elementary, but, I think, in consequence better developed—the theory of value.

To anyone who comes over from the theory of value to the theory of money, there are a number of things which are

[1] A paper read at the London Economic Club, November 1934, and printed in *Economica*, February 1935. The reader is asked to bear in mind the fact that the paper was written to be read aloud, and to excuse certain pieces of mischief.

rather startling. Chief of these is the preoccupation of monetary theorists with a certain equation, which states that the
price of goods multiplied by the quantity of goods equals the
amount of money which is spent on them. This equation
crops up again and again, and it has all sorts of ingenious
little arithmetical tricks performed on it. Sometimes it comes
out as $MV = PT$; and once, in its most stupendous trans-
figuration, it blossomed into $P = \dfrac{E}{O} + \dfrac{I'-S}{R}$. Now we, of the
theory of value, are not unfamiliar with this equation, and
there was a time when we used to attach as much importance
to it as monetary theorists seem to do still. This was in the
middle of the last century, when we used to talk about value
being 'a ratio between demand and supply'. Even now, we
accept the equation, and work it, more or less implicitly, into
our systems. But we are rather inclined to take it for granted,
since it is rather tautologous, and since we have found that
another equation, not alternative to the quantity equation,
but complementary with it, is much more significant. This
is the equation which states that the relative value of two
commodities depends upon their relative marginal utility.

Now, to an *ingénu*, who comes over to monetary theory, it
is extremely trying to be deprived of this sheet-anchor. It
was marginal utility that really made sense of the theory of
value; and to come to a branch of economics which does
without marginal utility altogether! No wonder there are
such difficulties and such differences! What is wanted is a
'marginal revolution'!

That is my suggestion. But I know that it will meet with
apparently crushing objections. I shall be told that the suggestion has been tried out before. It was tried by Wicksell,
and though it led to interesting results, it did not lead to a
marginal utility theory of money. It was tried by Mises,
and led to the conclusion that money is a ghost of gold—
because, so it appeared, money as such has no marginal utility.[1]

[1] A more subtle form of the same difficulty appears in the work of
Marshall and his followers. They were aware that money ought to be

The suggestion has a history, and its history is not encouraging.

This would be enough to frighten one off, were it not for two things. Both in the theory of value and in the theory of money there have been developments in the twenty or thirty years since Wicksell and Mises wrote. And these developments have considerably reduced the barriers that blocked their way.

In the theory of value, the work of Pareto, Wicksteed, and their successors, has broadened and deepened our whole conception of marginal utility. We now realize that the marginal utility analysis is nothing else than a general theory of choice, which is applicable whenever the choice is between alternatives that are capable of quantitative expression. Now money is obviously capable of quantitative expression, and therefore the objection that money has no marginal utility must be wrong. People do choose to have money rather than other things, and therefore, in the relevant sense, money must have a marginal utility.

But merely to call that marginal utility X, and then proceed to draw curves, would not be very helpful. Fortunately the developments in monetary theory to which I alluded come to our rescue.

Mr. Keynes's *Treatise*, so far as I have been able to discover, contains at least three theories of money. One of them is the Savings and Investment theory, which, as I hinted, seems to me only a quantity theory much glorified. One of them is a Wicksellian natural rate theory. But the third is

subjected to marginal utility analysis; but they were so dominated by the classical conception of money as a 'veil' (which is valid enough at a certain level of approximation) that they persisted in regarding the demand for money as a demand for the things which money can buy—'real balances'. As a result of this, their invocation of marginal utility remained little more than a pious hope. For they were unable to distinguish, on marginal utility lines, between the desire to save and the desire to hoard; and they necessarily overlooked that indeterminateness in the 'real balance' (so important in some applications of monetary theory), which occurs when the prices of consumption goods are expected to change. On the other hand, I must admit that some versions of the Marshallian theory come very close to what I am driving at. Cf. Lavington, *English Capital Market*, ch. vi.

altogether much more interesting. It emerges when Mr. Keynes begins to talk about the price-level of investment goods; when he shows that this price-level depends upon the relative preference of the investor—to hold bank-deposits or to hold securities. Here at last we have something which to a value theorist looks sensible and interesting! Here at last we have a choice at the margin! And Mr. Keynes goes on to put substance into our X, by his doctrine that the relative preference depends upon the 'bearishness' or 'bullishness' of the public, upon their relative desire for liquidity or profit.

My suggestion may, therefore, be reformulated. It seems to me that this third theory of Mr. Keynes really contains the most important part of his theoretical contribution; that here, at last, we have something which, on the analogy (the appropriate analogy) of value theory, does begin to offer a chance of making the whole thing easily intelligible; that it is from this point, not from velocity of circulation, natural rate of interest, or Saving and Investment, that we ought to start in constructing the theory of money. But in saying this, I am being more Keynesian than Keynes; I must endeavour to defend my position in detail.

II

The essence of the method I am proposing is that we should take the position of an individual at a particular point of time, and inquire what determines the precise quantity of money which he will desire to hold. But even to this simple formulation of the problem it is necessary to append two footnotes.

1. *Point of Time.* We are dealing with an individual decision to hold money *or* something else, and such a decision is always made at a point of time. It is only by concentrating on decisions made at particular points of time that we can apply the theory of value to the problem at all. A very large amount of current controversy about money seems to me to be due to the attempt, superficially natural, but, in fact, highly inconvenient, to establish a close relation between the demand

for money and *income*. Now the simple consideration that the decision to hold money is always made at a point of time shows that the connexion between income and the demand for money must always be indirect. And in fact the whole conception of income is so intricate and beset by so many perplexing difficulties, that the establishment of any connexion with income ought only to be hoped for at a late stage of investigation.[1]

2. *Money*. What sort of money are we considering? For the present, any sort of money. The following analysis will apply equally whether we think of money as notes, or bank deposits, or even metallic coins. It is true that with a metallic currency there is an ordinary commodity demand for the money substance to be considered, but it is relatively unimportant for most of our purposes. Perhaps it will be best if we take as our standard case that of a pure paper currency in a community where there are no banks. What follows has much wider application in reality. Only I would just ask you to keep this standard case in mind, since by using it as a basis for discussion, we may be able to save time a little.

An individual's decision to hold so much money means that he prefers to hold that amount of money, rather than either less or more. Now what are the precise contents of these displaced alternatives? He could reduce his holding of money in three ways:

1. By spending, i.e. buying something, it does not matter what;
2. By lending money to someone else;
3. By paying off debts which he owes to someone else.

He can increase his holding of money in three corresponding ways:

1. By selling something else which he owns;
2. By borrowing from someone else;

[1] Cf. Lindahl, *The Concept of Income* (Essays in honour of Gustav Cassel).

3. By demanding repayment of money which is owed by someone else.

This classification is, I think, complete. All ways of changing one's holding of money can be reduced to one of these classes or a combination of two of them—purchase or sale, the creation of new debts or the extinction of old.

If a person decides to hold money, it is implied that he prefers to do this rather than to adopt any of these three alternatives. But how is such a preference possible?

A preference for holding money instead of spending it on consumption goods presents no serious difficulty, for it is obviously the ordinary case of a preference for future satisfactions over present. At any moment, an individual will not usually devote the whole of his available resources to satisfying present wants—a part will be set aside to meet the needs of the future.

The critical question arises when we look for an explanation of the preference for holding money rather than capital goods. For capital goods will ordinarily yield a positive rate of return, which money does not. What has to be explained is the decision to hold assets in the form of barren money, rather than of interest- or profit-yielding securities. And obviously just the same question arises over our second and third types of utilization. So long as rates of interest are positive, the decision to hold money rather than lend it, or use it to pay off old debts, is apparently an unprofitable one.

This, as I see it, is really the central issue in the pure theory of money. Either we have to give an explanation of the fact that people do hold money when rates of interest are positive, or we have to evade the difficulty somehow. It is the great traditional evasions which have led to Velocities of Circulation, Natural Rates of Interest, *et id genus omne*.[1]

[1] I do not wish to deny that these concepts have a use in their appropriate place—that is to say, in particular applications of monetary theory. But it seems to me that they are a nuisance in monetary theory itself, that they offer no help in elucidating the general principles of the working of money.

Of course, the great evaders would not have denied that there must be some explanation of the fact. But they would have to put it down to 'frictions', and since there was no adequate place for frictions in the rest of their economic theory, a theory of money based on frictions did not seem to them a promising field for economic analysis.

This is where I disagree. I think we have to look the frictions in the face, and see if they are really so refractory after all. This will, of course, mean that we cannot allow them to go to sleep under so vague a title.

III

The most obvious sort of friction, and undoubtedly one of the most important, is the cost of transferring assets from one form to another. This is of exactly the same character as the cost of transfer which acts as a certain impediment to change in all parts of the economic system; it doubtless comprises subjective elements as well as elements directly priced. Thus a person is deterred from investing money for short periods, partly because of brokerage charges and stamp duties, partly because it is not worth the bother.

The net advantage to be derived from investing a given quantity of money consists of the interest or profit earned less the cost of investment. It is only if this net advantage is expected to be positive (i.e. if the expected rate of interest $\pm$ capital appreciation or depreciation, is greater than the cost of investment) that it will pay to undertake the investment.

Now, since the expected interest increases both with the quantity of money to be invested and with the length of time for which it is expected that the investment will remain untouched, while the costs of investment are independent of the length of time, and (as a whole) will almost certainly increase at a diminishing rate as the quantity of money to be invested increases, it becomes clear that with any given level of costs of investment, it will not pay to invest money for less than a certain period, and in less than certain quantities. It will be profitable to hold assets for short periods, and in relatively small quantities, in monetary form.

Thus, so far as we can see at present, the amount of money a person will desire to hold depends upon three factors: the dates at which he expects to make payments in the future, the cost of investment, and the expected rate of return on investment. The further ahead the future payments, the lower the cost of investment, and the higher the expected rate of return on invested capital—the lower will be the demand for money.

However, this statement is not quite accurate. For although all these factors may react on the demand for money, they may be insufficient to determine it closely. Since the quantity of available money must generally rise to some minimum before it is profitable to invest it at all, and further investment will then proceed by rather discontinuous jumps for a while, we shall expect to find the demand for money on the part of private individuals, excepting the very well-to-do, fairly insensitive to changes of this sort. But this does not mean that they are unimportant. For among those who are likely to be sensitive, we have to reckon, not only the well-to-do, but also all businessmen who are administering capital which is not solely their own private property. And this will give us, in total, a good deal of sensitivity.

IV

Our first list of factors influencing the demand for money—the expected rate of interest, the cost of investment, and the expected period of investment—does, therefore, isolate some factors which are really operative; but even so, it is not a complete list. For we have also to take into account the fact, which is in reality of such enormous importance, that people's expectations are never precise expectations of the kind we have been assuming. They do not say to themselves 'this £100 I shall not want until 1 June' or 'this investment will yield 3·7 per cent.'; or, if they do, it is only a kind of shorthand. Their expectations are always, in fact, surrounded by a certain penumbra of doubt; and the density of that penumbra is of immense importance for the problem we are considering.

The risk-factor comes into our problem in two ways: first, as affecting the expected period of investment; and second, as affecting the expected net yield of investment. There are certain differences between its ways of operation on these two lines; but, as we shall see, the resultant effects are broadly similar.

Where risk is present, the *particular* expectation of a riskless situation is replaced by a band of possibilities, each of which is considered more or less probable. It is convenient to represent these probabilities to oneself, in statistical fashion, by a mean value, and some appropriate measure of dispersion. (No single measure will be wholly satisfactory, but here this difficulty may be overlooked.) Roughly speaking, we may assume that a change in mean value with constant dispersion has much the same sort of effect as a change in the particular expectations we have been discussing before. The peculiar problem of risk therefore reduces to an examination of the consequences of a change in dispersion. Increased dispersion means increased uncertainty.

If, therefore, our individual, instead of knowing (or thinking he knows) that he will not want his £100 till 1 June becomes afflicted by increased uncertainty; that is to say, while still thinking that 1 June is the most likely date, he now thinks that it will be very possible that he will want it before, although it is also very possible that he will not want it till after; what will be the effect on his conduct? Let us suppose that when the date was certain, the investment was marginal —in the sense that the expected yield only just outweighed the cost of investment. With uncertainty introduced in the way we have described, the investment now offers a chance of larger gain, but it is offset by an equal chance of equivalent loss. In this situation, I think we are justified in assuming that he will become less willing to undertake the investment.

If this is so, uncertainty of the period for which money is free will ordinarily act as a deterrent to investment. It should be observed that uncertainty may be increased, either by a change in objective facts on which estimates are based, or in the psychology of the individual, if his temperament changes in such a way as to make him less inclined to bear risks.

To turn now to the other uncertainty—uncertainty of the yield of investment. Here again we have a penumbra; and here again we seem to be justified in assuming that spreading of the penumbra, increased dispersion of the possibilities of yield, will ordinarily be a deterrent to investment. Indeed, without assuming this to be the normal case, it would be impossible to explain some of the most obvious of the observed facts of the capital market. This sort of risk, therefore, will ordinarily be another factor tending to increase the demand for money.

V

So far the effect of risk seems fairly simple; an increase in the risk of investment will act like a fall in the expected rate of net yield; an increase in the uncertainty of future out-payments will act like a shortening of the time which is expected to elapse before those out-payments; and all will ordinarily tend to increase the demand for money. But although this is what it comes down to in the end, the detailed working of the risk-factor is not so simple; and since these further complications have an important bearing upon monetary problems, we cannot avoid discussing them here.

It is one of the peculiarities of risk that the total risk incurred when more than one risky investment is undertaken, does not bear any simple relation to the risk involved in each of the particular investments taken separately. In most cases, the 'law of large numbers' comes into play (quite how, cannot be discussed here), so that the risk incurred by undertaking a number of separate risky investments will be less than that which would have been incurred if the same total capital had been invested altogether in one direction. When the number of separate investments is very large, the total risk may sometimes be reduced very low indeed.

Now in a world where cost of investment was negligible, everyone would be able to take considerable advantage of this sort of risk-reduction. By dividing up his capital into small portions, and spreading his risks, he would be able to insure himself against any large total risk on the whole amount. But in actuality, the cost of investment, making it definitely unprofitable to invest less than a certain minimum amount in any particular direction, closes the possibility of risk-reduction along these lines to all those who do not possess the command over considerable quantities of capital. This has two consequences.

On the one hand, since most people do not possess sufficient resources to enable them to take much advantage of the law of large numbers, and since even the large capitalist cannot annihilate his risks altogether in this manner, there will be a tendency to spread capital over a number of investments, not for this purpose, but for another. By investing only a proportion of total assets in risky enterprises, and investing the remainder in ways which are considered more safe, it will be possible for the individual to adjust his whole risk-situation to that which he most prefers, more closely than he could do by investing in any single enterprise. It will be possible, for example, for him to feel fairly certain that in particular unfavourable eventualities he will not lose more than a certain amount. And, since, both with an eye on future commitments with respect to debt, and future needs for consumption, large losses will lay upon him a proportionately heavier burden than small losses, this sort of adjustment to the sort of chance of loss he is prepared to stand will be very well worth while.

We shall, therefore, expect to find our representative individual distributing his assets among relatively safe and relatively risky investments; and the distribution will be governed, once again, by the objective facts upon which he bases his estimates of risk, and his subjective preference for much or little risk-bearing.

On the other hand, those persons who have command of large quantities of capital, and are able to spread their risks, are not only able to reduce the risk on their own capital fairly low—they are also able to offer very good security for the investment of an extra unit along with the rest. If, therefore, they choose to become borrowers, they are likely to be very safe borrowers. They can, therefore, provide the safe investments which their fellow-citizens need.

In the absence of such safe investments, the ordinary individual would be obliged to keep a very considerable proportion of his assets in monetary form, since money would be the only safe way of holding assets. The appearance of such safe investments will act as a substitute for money in one of its uses, and therefore diminish the demand for money.

This particular function is performed, in a modern community, not only by banks, but also by insurance companies, investment trusts, and, to a certain (perhaps small) extent, even by large concerns of other kinds, through their prior charges. And, of course, to a very large extent indeed, it is performed by government stock of various kinds.

Banks are simply the extreme case of this phenomenon; they are enabled to go further than other concerns in the creation of money substitutes, because the security of their promises to pay is accepted generally enough for it to be possible to make payments in those promises. Bank deposits are, therefore, enabled to substitute money still further, because the cost of investment is reduced by a general belief in the absence of risk.

This is indeed a difference so great as to be properly regarded as a difference in kind; but it is useful to observe that the creation of bank credit is not really different in its economic effects from the fundamentally similar activities of other businesses and other persons. The significant thing is that the person who deposits money with a bank does not notice any change in his liquidity position; he considers the bank deposit to be as liquid as cash. The bank, on the other hand, finds itself more liquid, if it retains the whole amount of the cash deposited; if it does not wish to be more liquid, but seeks (for example) to restore a conventional reserve ratio, it will have to increase its investments. But substantially the same sort of thing happens when anyone, whose credit is much above the average, borrows. Here the borrowing is nearly always a voluntary act on the part of the borrower, which would not be undertaken unless he was willing to become less liquid than before; the fact that he has to pay interest on the loan means that he will be made worse off if he does not spend the proceeds. On the other hand, if the borrower's credit is good, the liquidity of the lender will not be very greatly impaired by his making the loan, so that his demand for money is likely to be at least rather less than it was before the loan was made. Thus the net effect of the loan is likely to be 'inflationary', in the sense that the purchase of capital goods or securities by the borrower is likely to be a more important affair than any sale of capital goods or securities by the lender, made necessary in order for the lender to restore his liquidity position.

Does it follow that all borrowing and lending is inflationary in this sense? I do not think so; for let us take the case when the borrower's credit is very bad, and the lender is only tempted to lend by the offer of a very high rate of interest. Then the impairment of the lender's liquidity position will be very considerable; and he may feel it necessary to sell rather less risky securities to an even greater capital sum in order to restore his liquidity position. Here the net effect would be 'deflationary'.

The practical conclusion of this seems to be that while *voluntary* borrowing and lending is at least a symptom of monetary expansion, and is thus likely to be accompanied by rising prices, 'distress borrowing' is an exception to this rule; and it follows, further, that the sort of stimulation to lending, by persuading people to make loans which they would not have made without persuasion (which was rather a feature of certain phases of the world depression), is a dubious policy—for the lenders, perhaps without realizing what they are doing, are very likely to try and restore their liquidity position, and so to offset, and perhaps more than offset, the expansive effects of the loan.

VI

It is now time for us to begin putting together the conclusions we have so far reached. Our method of analysis, it will have appeared, is simply an extension of the ordinary method of value theory. In value theory, we take a private individual's income and expenditure account; we ask which of the items in that account are under the individual's own control, and then how he will adjust these items in order to reach a most preferred position. On the production side, we make a similar analysis of the profit and loss account of the firm. My suggestion is that monetary theory needs to be based again upon a similar analysis, but this time, not of an income account, but of a capital account, a balance-sheet. We have to concentrate on the forces which make assets and liabilities what they are.

So as far as banking theory is concerned, this is really the method which is currently adopted; though the essence of the problem is there somewhat obscured by the fact that banks, in their efforts to reach their 'most preferred position' are hampered or assisted by the existence of conventional or legally obligatory reserve ratios. For theoretical purposes, this fact ought only to be introduced at a rather late stage; if that is done, then my suggestion can be expressed by saying that we ought to regard every individual in the community as being, on a small scale, a bank. Monetary theory becomes a sort of generalization of banking theory.

We shall have to draw up a sort of generalized balance-sheet, suitable for all individuals and institutions. It will have to be so generalized that many of the individual items will, in a great many cases, not appear. But that does not matter for our purposes. Such a generalized balance-sheet will presumably run much as follows:

Assets	*Liabilities*
Consumption goods —perishable	
Consumption goods —durable	
Money	
Bank deposits	
Short term debts	Short term debts
Long term debts	Long terms debts
Stocks and shares	
Productive equipment (including goods in process)	

We have been concerned up to the present with an analysis (very sketchy, I am afraid) of the equilibrium of this balance sheet. This analysis has at least shown that the relative size of the different items on this balance-sheet is governed mainly by anticipation of the yield of investments and of risks.[1] It is these anticipations which play a part here corresponding to the part played by prices in value theory.[2]

Now the fact that our 'equilibrium' is here determined by subjective factors like anticipations, instead of objective factors like prices, means that this purely theoretical study of money can never hope to reach results so tangible and precise

[1] As we have seen, these risks are as much a matter of the period of investment as of the yield. For certain purposes this is very important. Thus, in the case of that kind of investment which consists in the starting of actual processes of production, the yield which is expected if the process can be carried through may be considerable; but the yield if the process has to be interrupted will be large and negative. Uncertainty of the period for which resources are free will therefore have a very powerful effect in interrupting production. Short-run optimism will usually be enough to start a Stock Exchange boom; but to start an industrial boom relatively long-run optimism is necessary.

[2] I am aware that too little is said in this paper about the liabilities side of the above balance-sheet. A cursory examination suggests that the same forces which work through the assets side work through the liabilities side in much the same way. But this certainly requires further exploration.

as those which value theory in its more limited field can hope to attain. If I am right, the whole problem of applying monetary theory is largely one of deducing changes in anticipations from the changes in objective data which call them forth. Obviously, this is not an easy task, and, above all, it is not one which can be performed in a mechanical fashion. It needs judgement and knowledge of business psychology much more than sustained logical reasoning. The armchair economist will be bad at it, but he can at least begin to realize the necessity for it, and learn to co-operate with those who can do it better than he can.

However, I am not fouling my own nest; I do not at all mean to suggest that economic theory comes here to the end of its resources. When once the connexion between objective facts and anticipations has been made, theory comes again into its rights; and it will not be able to complain of a lack of opportunities.

Nevertheless, it does seem to me most important that, when considering these further questions, we should be well aware of the gap which lies behind us, and that we should bring out very clearly the assumptions which we are making about the genesis of anticipations. For this does seem to be the only way in which we can overcome the extraordinary theoretical differences of recent years, which are, I think, very largely traceable to this source.

VII

Largely, but not entirely; or rather a good proportion of them seem to spring from a closely related source, which is yet not quite identical with the first. When we seek to apply to a changing world any particular sort of individual equilibrium, we need to know how the individual will respond, not only to changes in the price-stimuli, or anticipation-stimuli, but also to a change in his total wealth.[1] How will he dis-

[1] The amount of money demanded depends upon three groups or factors: (1) the individual's subjective preferences for holding money of

tribute an increment (or decrement) of wealth—supposing, as we may suppose, that this wealth is measured in monetary terms?

It may be observed that this second problem has an exact counterpart in value theory. Recent work in that field has shown the importance of considering carefully, not only how the individual reacts to price-changes, but also how he reacts to changes in his available expenditure. Total wealth, in our present problem, plays just the same part as total expenditure in the theory of value.

In the theory of money, what we particularly want to know is how the individual's demand for money will respond to a change in his total wealth—that is to say, in the value of his net assets. Not seeing any *a priori* reason why he should react in one way rather than another, monetary theorists have often been content to make use of the simplest possible assumption—that the demand for money will be increased in the same proportion as total net assets have increased.[1] But this is a very arbitrary assumption; and it may be called in question, partly for analytical reasons, and partly because it seems to make the economic system work much too smoothly to account for observed fact. As one example of this excessive smoothness, I may instance the classical theory of international payments; as another, Mr. Harrod's views on the 'Expansion of Bank Credit' which have recently been interesting the readers of *Economica* and of the *Economist*.[2] It would hardly be too much to say that one observed fact alone is sufficient to prove that this assumption cannot be universally

other things; (2) his wealth; (3) his anticipations of future prices and risks. Changes in the demand for money affect present prices, but present prices affect the demand for money mainly through their effect on wealth and on price-anticipations.

[1] Of course, they say 'income'. But in this case 'income' can only be strictly interpreted as 'expected income'. And in most of the applications which are made, this works out in the same way as the assumption given above.

[2] The above was written before reading Mr. Harrod's rejoinder to Mr. Robertson. As I understand him, Mr. Harrod is now only maintaining that the expansion of bank credit *may* work smoothly. With that I am in no disagreement.

true (let us hope and pray that it is sometimes true, never-theless)—the fact of the trade cycle. For if it were true, the monetary system would always exhibit a quite straight-forward kind of stability; a diminished demand for money on the part of some people would raise the prices of capital goods and securities, and this would raise the demand for money on the part of the owners of those securities. Similarly an in-creased demand for money would lower prices, and this would lower the demand for money elsewhere. The whole thing would work out like an ordinary demand and supply diagram. But it is fairly safe to say that we do not find this straightforward stability in practice.

The analytical reason why this sort of analysis is unsatis-factory is the following: The assumption of increased wealth leading to a proportionately increased demand for money is only plausible so long as the value of assets has increased, but other things have remained equal. Now, as we have seen, the other things which are relevant to this case are not prices (as in the theory of value) but anticipations, of the yield of invest-ment and so on. And since these anticipations must be based upon objective facts, and an unexpected increase in wealth implies a change in objective facts, of a sort very likely to be relevant to the anticipations, it is fairly safe to assume that very many of the changes in wealth with which we are con-cerned will be accompanied by a change in anticipations. If this is so, the assumption of proportionate change in the demand for money loses most of its plausibility.

For if we assume (this is jumping over my gap, so I must emphasize that it is only an assumption) that an increase in wealth will very often be accompanied by an upward revision of expectations of yield, then the change will set in motion at least one tendency which is certain to diminish the demand for money. Taking this into account *as well as* the direct effect of the increase in wealth, the situation begins to look much less clear. For it must be remembered that our provisional assumption about the direct effect was only guess-work; there is no necessary reason why the direct effect should increase the demand for money proportionately or even increase it at all. So, putting the two together, it looks perfectly possible that the demand for money may either increase or diminish.

We are treading on thin ice; but the unpleasant possibilities which now begin to emerge are sufficiently plausible for their examination to be well worth while. What happens, to take a typical case, if the demand for money is independent of changes in wealth, so that neither an increase in wealth nor a diminution will affect the demand for money?

One can conceive of a sort of equilibrium in such a world, but it would be a hopelessly unstable equilibrium. For if any single person tried to increase his money holdings, and the supply of money was not increased, prices would all fall to zero. If any person tried to diminish his money holdings, prices would all become infinite. In fact, of course, if demand were so rigid, the system could only be kept going by a continuous and meticulous adaptation of the supply of money to the demand.

Further, in such a world, very curious results would follow from saving. A sudden increase in saving would leave some people (the owners of securities) with larger money balances than they had expected; other people (the producers of consumption goods) with smaller money balances. If, in their efforts to restore their money holdings, the owners of securities buy more securities, and the producers of consumption goods buy less consumption goods, a swing of prices, consumption goods prices falling, security prices rising, would set in, and might go on indefinitely. It could only be stopped, either by the owners of securities buying the services of producers, or by the producers selling securities. But there is no knowing when this would happen, or where prices would finally settle; for the assumption of a rigid demand for money snaps the connecting link between money and prices.

After this, we shall be fairly inured to shocks. It will not surprise us to be told that wage-changes will avail nothing to stop either an inflation or a deflation, and we shall be able to extend the proposition for ourselves to cover interference with

conventional or monopolistic prices of any kind, in any direction. But we shall be in a hurry to get back to business.

VIII

These exercises in the economics of an utterly unstable world
give us something too made to fit even our modern *Spät-
kapitalismus*; but the time which economists have spent on them
will not have been wasted if they have served as a corrective
to the too facile optimism engendered by the first assumption
we tried. Obviously, what we want is something between the
two—but not, I think, a mere splitting of the difference. This
would give the assumption that an increase in wealth always
raises the demand for money, but less than proportionately;
if we had time, it might be profitable to work out this case
in detail. It would allow for the possibility of considerable
fluctuations, but they would not be such absurd and hope-
less fluctuations as in the case of rigid demand.

However, I think we can do better than that. The assumption which seems to me most plausible, most consistent with
the whole trend of our analysis, and at the same time to lead
to results which at any rate look realistic, is one which stresses
the probable differences in the reactions of different members
of the community. We have already seen that a considerable
proportion of a community's monetary stock is always likely
to be in the hands of people who are obliged by their relative
poverty to be fairly insensitive to changes in anticipations.
For these people, therefore, most of the incentive to reduce
their demand for money when events turn out more favour-
ably will be missing; there seems no reason why we should
not suppose that they will generally react 'positively' to
changes in their wealth—that an increase in wealth will raise
their demand for money more or less proportionately, a fall in
their wealth will diminish it. But we must also allow for the
probability that other people are much more *sensitive*—that
an increase in wealth is not particularly likely to increase
their demand for money, and may very well diminish it.

If this is so, it would follow that where the sensitive trade together, price-fluctuations may start on very slight provocation; and once they are under way, the rather less sensitive would be enticed in. Stock exchange booms will pass over into industrial booms, if industrial entrepreneurs are also fairly sensitive; and, in exactly the same way, stock exchange depressions will pass into industrial depressions. But the insensitive are always there to act as a flywheel, defeating by their insensitivity both the exaggerated optimism and the exaggerated pessimism of the sensitive class. How this comes about I cannot attempt to explain in detail, though it would be an interesting job, for one might be able to reconcile a good many apparently divergent theories. But it would lead us too deeply into Cycle theory—I will only say that I think the period of fluctuation turns out to depend, in rather complex fashion, upon the distribution of sensitivity and the distribution of production periods between industrial units.

Instead, I may conclude with two general reflections.

If it is the insensitive people who preserve the stability of capitalism, people who are insensitive (you will remember) largely because for them the costs of transferring assets are large relative to the amount of assets they control, then the development of capitalism, by diminishing these costs, is likely to be a direct cause of increasing fluctuations. It reduces costs in two ways: by technical devices (of which banks are only one example), and by instilling a more 'capitalistic' spirit, which looks more closely to profit, and thus reduces subjective costs. In doing these things, capitalism is its own enemy, for it imperils that stability without which it breaks down.

Lastly, it seems to follow that when we are looking for policies which make for economic stability, we must not be led aside by a feeling that monetary troubles are due to 'bad' economic policy, in the old sense, that all would go well if we reverted to free trade and *laisser-faire*. In so doing, we are no better than the Thebans who ascribed the plague to blood-guiltiness, or the supporters of Mr. Roosevelt who expect to reach recovery through reform.[1] There is no reason why policies which tend to economic welfare, statically considered, should also tend to monetary stability. Indeed, the presumption is rather the other way round. A tariff, for example, may be a very good instrument of recovery on occasion, for precisely the reason which free-traders deplore; that it harms a great many people a little for the conspicuous benefit of a few. That may be just the sort of measure we want.

These will be unpalatable conclusions; but I think we must face the possibility that they are true. They offer the economist a pretty hard life, for he, at any rate, will not be able to have a clear conscience either way, over many of the alternatives he is called upon to consider. His ideals will conflict and he will not be able to seek an easy way out by sacrificing either.

[1] Or, as I might have said if I had been writing in 1967, the supporters of Dr. Prebitsch who seek, by 'structural' reforms that may otherwise be very desirable, to control the inflations that are endemic in South America.

5

THE YIELD ON CONSOLS[1]

It was in 1750 that Henry Pelham (not one of the more distinguished of British prime ministers, if he was a prime minister) established his main title to fame by shepherding the National Debt, then largely owing to certain big corporations, into that readily marketable 3 per cent. stock, which became known as Consols.[2] In so doing, he created an economic statistic (the Yield on Consols) which now extends, with fair comparability, over a period of more than two hundred years; enabling us to make long-period, or in the strict sense secular comparisons, such as are hardly possible in any other field of economic study. There are here no changes of base, no corrections needed for changes in population or in money values; for a rate of interest, being a pure ratio, can be measured on the same scale throughout. A chart of the Yield on Consols, extending from Pelham's time right up to the present is shown in Fig. 4.[3]

[1] A revised and modernized form of a paper read to the Manchester Statistical Society in March 1958, and subsequently submitted in evidence to the Radcliffe Committee.
[2] For a detailed account of the Pelham 'conversion', see P. G. Dickson, *The Financial Revolution in England* (1967).
[3] I have put the chart together from the following sources. Up to 1800, T. S. Ashton, *Economic History of England* (*the Eighteenth Century*), p. 251. From 1800 to 1833, J. Vansommer, *Tables of Three per cent Consols* (1834), lent to me by Professor Ashton. From 1833 to 1848 I have used the Gibson table printed in A. W. Kirkcaldy, *British Public Finances, 1914–21*. From 1849 to 1910, T. T. Williams, 'Rate of Discount and Price of Consols' (*Statistical Journal, 1912*). From 1910 to 1920, *Bankers' Magazine*. After 1920 the figures are readily available in *Statistical Abstracts* and such like.

It is doubtless the case that these very varied sources are not always comparable in detail; I would not swear, for instance, that some of the figures I have used are not annual averages, while some may be end-of-year figures. But I am not sure that the table in Mitchell and Deane, *British Historical Statistics*, p. 455, is much more firmly based. I have

[cont. on p. 85

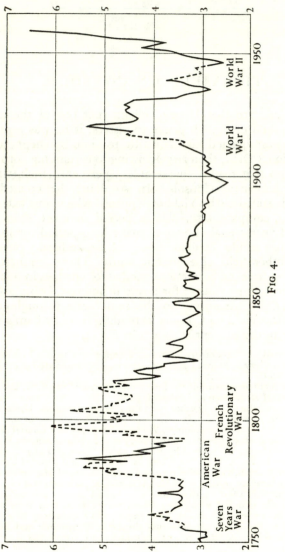

FIG. 4.

But before we can turn to consider any particular features of the story that is unfolded on the Chart, I must insert a number of warnings. It must not be taken for granted that the Yield, as shown, is identical with the Rate of Interest (the Long-Term Rate of Interest) as that expression is used in economic textbooks. The Pure Long-Term Rate should be a rate that is paid by a borrower of unimpeachable solvency (so that there is no default risk) for a loan of indefinite duration. It can hardly be maintained that at all points of this majestic sequence, the Yield on Consols does satisfy these exacting requirements. To assume that in the bad years (in 1781, in 1798, in 1917, or even in 1940) there was absolutely no default risk, is perhaps going rather far. But it is much more important that there are several dates at which the other condition quite clearly fails to hold. There has always been a technical possibility of conversion at some future date, to a lower (nominal) rate of interest; so long as the nominal rate remained at 3 per cent., this possibility did become, from time to time, quite serious. Then in 1888 the conversion actually occurred. (The Yield, as shown on the Chart, is, of course, adjusted accordingly.) At no time since the Goschen conversion has a conversion to less than his 2½ per cent. looked seriously possible, so that since 1888 the correspondence with a theoretical Long-Term Rate should have been closer. Nevertheless (for reasons which the chart itself makes intelligible) the Yield on Consols has become less representative of the yield on Government debt as a whole than it was in the nineteenth century. These very long bonds, which were then the main form of Government Debt outstanding, are now (especially since the second of our wars) a very small part of the total volume of Debt which is on the market.

It is also important, before we start on our main inquiry, to be clear about the distinction between the Pure Rate of Interest, as just defined, and what economists often call the

therefore left the original chart which was given in the Manchester paper. I have no doubt that it is good enough for the uses that I want to make of it.

Rate of Interest, which is the Representative Rate at which business can raise capital. This latter can, of course, be no more than an average or index-number, with the usual difficulties of index-numbers attaching to it. It cannot be identified with any single rate, such as the Yield on Consols, though we may sometimes allow ourselves to think of it as a Pure Rate, plus (or even conceivably minus) a risk-premium. There is some presumption that when the Pure Rate goes up, the Representative Rate goes up; but, especially when we remember that the Representative Rate should be influenced by the terms on which capital can be raised by the issue of ordinary shares, it may not be a strong presumption on all occasions. The 'risk-premium' (if that is the right word for it) may be very volatile. But even if we decide—as I am inclined to do—that movements in the Pure Rate of Interest are less important, in relation to the activity of industry, than economists used to suppose, they remain of much importance to everyone who has financial dealings—to bankers (in the widest sense), to trustees, and not least to those who are concerned with the finance of government itself.

We may now examine the Chart, which has been drawn (I may remark) with the years crushed rather closely together, but with percentage differences that sound small rather widely spread. This, I think, is appropriate, since if we convert the yields into their reciprocals (the *price* of Consols) the movements on the graph which look big really are big movements. A doubling of yield, such as took place (very nearly) between 1792 and 1798, between 1910 and 1917, and between 1947 and 1957, means that the price of the stock is halved. Over the range within which the figures move, we do (I think) get the right impression from the scale I have taken.

It is evident, from the most cursory glance, that the story which the Chart tells falls into three phases. The first is that of the Eighteenth-century Wars; the second that of the Long Peace from 1815 to 1914; the third is that of the Wars (and other disturbances) in our century. Though there were wars, such as the Crimean War and the Boer War, during the Long

Peace, they hardly cause a ripple on the Chart. The effects of the Eighteenth-century Wars and of the First World War are much alike. That of the Second World War, however, is quite a different story.[1]

Let us begin by considering the Three Wars (those beginning in 1776, 1792, and 1914) where a rather similar phenomenon seems to be repeated. There was in each case a sharp rise in the rate of interest, as the war developed; and in each case there was an Aftermath, during which there was a persistence of high rates (sometimes even higher than those in the war years) lasting after the war was over. The Aftermath of the War of American Independence lasted until 1791; it was hardly over (but it clearly was just over) before the next war started. The Aftermath of the Napoleonic War lasted at least until 1823; some might say until 1831. The Aftermath of the war of 1914 appears, from the Chart, to extend as far as the War Loan Conversion of 1932; but whether that is a right interpretation is one of the main things we have to consider. For it carries with it the question whether our present experience is also an Aftermath, different in character from its predecessors because of the different way in which the Second World War was financed, or whether it is something more different still. This is in fact the question, with implications for the future rather than the past, to which my historical inquiry is leading up.

Looking, for the present, at the earlier Aftermaths alone, how do we explain them? Each of the Three Wars was financed by a large creation of long-term Debt. By throwing all this new Stock on to the market the Government had depressed the prices of its securities; new stockholders had had to be found (often in a hurry) who had not been willing to hold so much government debt at the old prices, for otherwise they would have bought it previously. The high interest rates that ruled at the end of each war could be read as a symptom of a condition in which the market was choked with government debt. In order that interest rates should

[1] War years are distinguished by dotting the line on the chart.

return to a normal level, it was necessary for that surplus, somehow or other, to be worked off. The time which was taken for the working-off is the duration of the Aftermath.

So much, I think, is really common ground; but when we ask how the 'working-off' was performed, we come to a difference between the views of post-Keynesian economists and their predecessors. On the older view, the obvious way out was to reduce the surplus by debt repayment; though since it is evident, as a matter of history, that this is not the way out which was adopted in practice, an alternative had to be provided. Repayment of debt out of budget surpluses is government saving; the same end would be attained if others than government did the saving, for by saving the funds available for the purchase of the Stock would be increased. (There was a reinforcing idea that the saving was necessary in order to replace 'real capital' that had been destroyed in the war. But this is a singularly unconvincing idea with respect, at least, to the earlier wars; for it can hardly be doubted that during those wars the real capital of the Nation was being increased, and quite probably being increased at an exceptionally rapid rate. I put this point on one side, for the notion that the working off of the surplus debt required extra saving can be stated in a manner which does not involve us in these historical absurdities.)

Nevertheless, however this argument is expressed, it can at the most contain a part of the truth; it misses the main key to what actually happened. We must look at the Debt (the holding of the Debt) in its proper context. We do this if we consider what the *asset structure* of the public would have been like at the close of one of these wars. (By this *asset structure* I mean a consolidated balance-sheet of all businesses and persons in the country, including banks, or such banks as there were, but *excluding* the Government.) The volume of Government Debt, included among these assets, would (as stated) have been abnormally large; it would have been large, that is, *relatively to* the other items in the balance-sheet. These other items would have included some which were less liquid than the (marketable) Debt—typically the real capital goods in the possession of the public, or (if we like to arrange our balance-sheet in that manner) the 'industrial' securities and obligations which 'represent' the real goods. The other items would, however, have also included some which were more liquid than the Debt, typically cash itself. On this more complete way of regarding the problem, the surplus in the supply of Government Debt could have been absorbed, either by an expansion in the whole stock of assets (so that the Government Debt, so long as it remained unchanged in magnitude, would come to occupy a smaller proportion of the whole); or alternatively by an increased willingness to hold Debt, so that a supply which had been felt to be excessive, was no longer felt to be excessive in the same way.

When the matter is looked at in this manner, it becomes apparent that an increase in the volume of real capital goods (the relatively illiquid end of the assets spectrum), such as would normally come about by a process of saving and investment, would itself be of little help with respect to the problem with which we are concerned. For if there was an expansion at that end, and no expansion (or no corresponding expansion) on the side of cash, the shortage of cash would become greater than ever; people would therefore try to *sell* their Government Debt in order to get more cash, and the rate of interest would rise still further. (This is the kind of thing that did happen in the post-war booms, with higher than war-time rates of interest, which are to be noticed at the end of some of our wars.) What would give relief would be an expansion of the cash base, or (what would have the same effect) the discovery of means by which the public could satisfy its needs for liquid cash with less cash than before. It is, I believe, in such directions as these that we must look for an explanation of the way in which the Aftermaths of high interest rates were brought to an end in the periods which followed the earlier wars.[1]

[1] It is indeed true that relief may come, not from an easing of the money supply, but from a fall in prices (of the real goods); with a lower

In the conditions of those times, such alleviation should indeed have been peculiarly simple. The basic *money* of the country was the gold coins that still circulated; the opportunities for economizing in the use of that money, by using it indirectly as a 'backing' for credit of various kinds, instead of using it as a direct medium of exchange, were enormous. High rates of interest, by increasing the profitability of such banking transactions, would give a direct stimulus to the expansion of credit. I do not think that it can be doubted that it was the expansion of banking, in the widest sense of that term, which came to the rescue, and brought the interest squeezes of the earlier Aftermaths to an end.

Further, once this process had begun, it would feed on itself. One of the interesting things which emerge from the Chart is the tendency for the Yield on Consols, when it was not being boosted by wars or their aftermaths, to sink, in all *normal* years during the first century of our story, to much the same level. In the seventeen-sixties, at 1790, and again from 1832 to 1875 (though in the latter period there are little ups and downs that can usually be traced to very identifiable causes), there is a distinct tendency for the rate to settle at something between 3 and 3½ per cent., and not to move outside that range. It is not difficult to see why this was. We are still in the age of 3 per cent. Consols; at this normal level Consols were 5–10 per cent. below par. If Consols had risen above par, there was a possibility of conversion; so that as the par level was approached, there was little chance of a capital gain from appreciation, but always (of course) the chance of a loss. The gap between the actual rate and 3 per cent. may thus be said to have represented a normal risk-premium. If, on the other hand, the Yield was much in excess of 3 per cent. (as it was in the Aftermath periods), there was a prospect of a capital gain of considerable magnitude, once

price-level a given supply of money will go further. Even when the market is glutted with debt, interest can come down if there is a sufficiently severe and sufficiently prolonged slump. This has relevance to the case of the nineteen-thirties, but while dealing with the earlier experience I think I am justified in leaving it out of account.

confidence was restored, so that people began to anticipate a return of the interest rate to this normal level. This speculative force could hardly begin to operate until the movement towards 'equilibrium' had begun, so that it does not permit us to dispense with the other explanation of why the movement took place; it does, however, help to explain why it was the kind of movement that it was—why it went so far and no further.

I must pass on to the next chapter.[1] This is the fascinating episode in the later nineteenth century when the Yield on Consols broke through the 3 per cent. barrier, actually falling (after the Goschen conversion) to a minimum of $2\frac{1}{2}$ per cent. in 1895, the lowest point of all time, for it was not beaten (as an annual average) even by Dr. Dalton! This particular year was a depression year, and the effects of the Trade Cycle on my curve are a matter that I shall leave on one side for the moment; they are indeed remarkably small during the whole of the nineteenth century. It is the long period of low interest rates that lasted, across fluctuations in trade, from about 1880 to 1910, which is the matter on which I want to fix attention.

Once the conversion had occurred, the barrier was of course removed; but this does not explain how it was possible to remove the barrier. Nor does it explain why it was possible for such low interest rates to rule in that period, and not later. In fact, if we go back to the earlier years of the Long Peace, we can find earlier occasions when rates began to fall in such a way as to make conversion look momentarily possible; but these low rates were not held. It was the long period of low rates before 1888 which made conversion possible; it seems reasonable to suppose that the same forces

[1] I skip discussion of some particular problems of the Napoleonic War and its aftermath: the change from the financial methods of Pitt to those of Petty and Vansittart, with consequent relaxation of the interest squeeze, and the (partly consequential) depreciation of Bank money. It is, however, worth observing that this change, between the two parts of that twenty years' war, was to some extent a rehearsal for the corresponding change between the two wars of this century.

which began to lower rates in that period lowered them still further later on. What were those forces?

At the point in the story we have now reached, the total of Government Debt that was in existence was no larger than in 1817, while the capacity of the economy to carry that Debt had grown enormously. Government Debt was no longer in excess supply; it had really become rather scarce. The scarcity would doubtless have shown itself earlier than it did, had it not been for the appearance of another financial asset which developed, in the eyes of the market, a rather similar quality—the Railway Bond. It was Government Stock plus Railway Bonds which was being held (say at mid-century) in something of the same position in the combined balance-sheet (of the private sector, now, of course, excluding the railway companies) as had previously been occupied by Government Stock alone. It was possible for all this to be held, not too inconveniently, because of the growth of credit. But as the Railway Age began to peter out, so that the rate of expansion of the railway debt began to diminish, the credit expansion took another step forward, through the growth of deposit banking (especially after 1858). This would force down the yield on Consols, and keep it low, *provided it was allowed to have its effect in an uninterrupted manner*. By the eighteen-eighties this last condition was realized; it had not been realized before, and that (I believe) is the reason why the period of very low rates did not start before. But this is a controversial matter; the point of view that I am adopting requires some defence, and some explanation.[1]

Throughout the whole of its long history, the price of Consols has been determined by supply and demand; though Government has often intervened so as to influence the price (by its own buying or selling), there has been no price control —the price has always been determined on the market. Now the price of any durable commodity that is so determined may

---

[1] I have discussed this matter on earlier occasions; see my *Value and Capital*, ch. xi, and my review-article on Hawtrey's *Century of Bank Rate* (Manchester School 1939).

be regarded as being set by the valuation which is put upon it by the marginal holder; and this, in its turn, is a matter of comparison between the net advantage of holding wealth in this form and the net advantage of holding it in any other form that may be on offer. The net advantage has other components ('convenience and security' to use Marshall's expression) as well as the yield; but the yield of the security, with due allowance for the probability of capital appreciation or depreciation, is the consideration to which we must mainly look. That, in particular, is the case of the pure speculator, who is in the market today and out tomorrow; his expectation of what the price will be in the near future is his sole concern. A less speculative investor, who nevertheless contemplates the possibility that he will want to sell at some (unknown) future date, must also look at running yield (the yield shown on our Chart); but he is not only affected by running yield, he is also affected by the sort of price which he expects to find ruling in the 'foreseeable' future. If he feels that this latter price can be foreseen fairly safely, he will be more willing to hold than he will be if he considers that there is serious chance of depreciation. Taking these cases together, we may say that in general the willingness to hold Stock depends on the running yield and on the expectation (with due allowance for risk) of the future price of the security.[1]

For certain holders, though not (of course) for all, one alternative to the holding of a long bond (such as Consols) would be the holding of some similar stock of shorter maturity —even, it may be, a very short obligation, such as a bill. Thus if bill rates are high (usually implying that Bank Rate is high), there will be less incentive to hold bonds. But, so long as expectations of future bond prices are unaffected (and it is possible that they may be almost unaffected, if the high bill rates are expected to be quite temporary), a very small

---

[1] Strictly speaking, it is the expectation of the marginal investor which matters. That is why an increase in the volume of the debt has itself a tendency to depress prices; investors must be tempted to come in whose expectations are less favourable, or who are less willing to hold stock for some other reason.

depreciation in bond prices will offer the prospect of a capital gain that is sufficient to compensate for a big apparent difference, between bill and bond, in running yield. That is why the 7 per cent. Bank Rate of 1866 (for instance) had no more effect on the yield of Consols than appears from my Chart. All the same, it did have some effect—more, I think, than the arithmetical effect just mentioned. After all, when Bank Rate is raised to crisis height, no one knows how long the crisis will last. The high Bank Rate must have some effect on expectations; that is why the actual effect is bound to be greater than the arithmetical effect.

This indeed is a 'psychological' matter; the effect will be greater the greater the crisis *appears*. Accordingly, if there has been a lot of experience of such crises, the purchaser of a bond is liable to be influenced by the fear that the time when he wants to sell (generally unknown at the time of purchase) will turn out, when it comes, to be a time of crisis; and even if he himself is not directly influenced by that particular risk, he will base his expectations on experience which has itself been affected by such expectations on the part of other people. It follows, I think, that experience of financial crises (with high short-term rates) is itself a factor tending to raise long-term rates, for quite a time after each crisis is over.[1]

---

[1] In my previous attempts (cited in a former note) to state this argument more formally, there were various simplifications which may have invited misunderstanding. I do not for a moment deny that the speculative purchaser of a long bond needs only to compare the yield on that bond (including expected capital appreciation over the shortest period in the future) with the similarly calculated yield on a security of shorter maturity. For he can get out again whenever he chooses. But if we suppose that he bases his expectations of future *bond* prices on the assumption that the market in general (consisting of himself and persons like himself) will go on behaving on the same principles as those on which he is at present behaving, he must assume that if the high bill rates continue, the price of bonds will continue to be depressed. Thus his expectation can be *analysed* into an expectation of the behaviour of short rates. Since (with a developed banking system) it is in most cases the short rates which are most directly determined by conditions outside the market, it simplifies the analysis, and does not vitiate its conclusions, to treat the expectations of investors *as if they were* expectations of short rates. But there is nothing inevitable about this; there are cases (such as that of the U.S. market

Now it is well known that the middle years of the nine-teenth century were a period of exceptionally acute financial crises; the effects of these crises (in 1847, 1857, and 1866) can be observed on our Chart. After 1866 there was a long period in which the economic fluctuations (which continued to occur) did not issue in the same kind of *financial* crisis. On the theory just sketched, it was the violent crises of the earlier period which were the reason why the period of low interest rates did not set in earlier. By 1880, the risk of these (temporary) falls in the price of Consols seemed much diminished. The tide of credit expansion was flowing smoothly and evenly, perhaps in part just because the pace of real economic development was less hectic; the weight of money that was pushing the long-term rate down was less impeded by risks, so that the 3 per cent. line was decisively crossed.

I have said nothing, so far, about international repercus-sions. It seemed (but perhaps I was wrong) that it was justi-fiable to neglect them, in an outline analysis, so long as I was concerned with the first part of my story; but at the point I have now reached it would clearly be wrong to do so any longer. The world money market (and capital market) was forming; that these low interest rates could be established in England, and could be maintained, in the face of this greater mobility of capital, is a remarkable sign of the finan-cial strength of the British economy at that date. The absence of financial crises is itself an indication of the strength of the (current) balance of payments; but it is also a sign of the con-fidence which was held internationally, in the strength of the British economy relatively to the economies of other coun-tries. Otherwise the low interest rates in England would have been sapped—as they evidently were sapped after 1900, when confidence in the development of other countries had increased so far as to induce a great expansion in British investment overseas. The upward movement from 1900 to

in the years just before 1953) which it would obviously be more convenient to analyse the other way.

1914 does not, I think, require (I shall certainly not give it) any more explanation than that.

I come, very belatedly, nearer to our own times. In the Aftermath of the nineteen-twenties, the 5 per cent. War Loan formed a *barrier* in much the same way as the Old 3 per cent. Consols had done before they were converted. It is, however, clear, on our principles, that this barrier should have been broken through much more quickly and easily than it was, if the general financial strength of the economy had been greater. The credit expansion which was required, in order that the great mass of War Debt could be easily carried, could not be allowed to occur, because of the weakness of sterling. It was not until the defence of sterling had been abandoned (September 1931) that the War Loan could be converted (June 1932); and that the quite new expectations of a radically altered situation could establish a Yield of less than 3 per cent. in 1935.

No doubt we have then come to a time (after 1932) when the Rate of Interest—even the Long-Term Rate, which is our concern here—has begun to be 'managed'; the question accordingly arises how far the low interest rates of the mid-thirties could be considered to be 'normal', even for those times. I think that for the maintenance of these low rates to have been possible, a number of conditions were necessary. I do not include among these conditions the continuance of a state of depression, for even in those days the continuance of depression was not really to be expected, and when interest rates were at their lowest (in 1935–6) trade was already picking up. The basic thing which was needed was a continuation of monetary ease, and an expectation that this ease would go on. But this had various implications. The monetary ease might have been ended by an outbreak of war, if war had been financed in the old way; as the war cloud drew nearer, the Yield did in fact rise. It might have been ended by an exchange crisis; the policy of putting exchange stability second to the maintenance of low interest rates was an essential condition of the 2 per cent. Bank Rate that ruled throughout. So long as this policy was maintained, that was a small risk. It might conceivably have been ended by a real boom; but there was then no reason to expect anything more than a boom which would have produced a temporary stringency, and that, as we have seen, need not, by earlier experience, have affected the long rate very much. So long as the pattern of expectations remained as I have been describing it, a 2 per cent. Bank Rate was bound to press down the long-term rate, even to fairly low levels.

I need not describe the remarkable methods by which the Second World War was in fact financed. Instead of flooding the market with long-term debt, the supply of shorts was expanded to keep pace with that of longs; under the impact of the new policy, the long-term rate actually fell, instead of rising as it had done on previous occasions. As a result, instead of ending the War with a surfeit of longs, we ended it with a surfeit of shorts, that continued, for years, to provide the fuel for post-war inflation. That is to say, the 'thirties' policy of monetary ease was carried right through the war into a different epoch. Now, however, instead of being associated with a floating exchange rate it was associated with an exchange that was supposed to be fixed. The floating exchange rate, which was one of the defences of the low interest rates of the thirties, was gone. During the war, and immediately after, its place was supplied by exchange control —and also, in some measure, by other controls. In the exceptional conditions of the time, that could work; but when the controls were relaxed, something had to give. One of the things that gave was the low interest rate.

And so we pass to the current situation, for which I have been trying to provide a background of history. The rise in the long-term rate since 1946 (as shown on the Chart) has been quite startling; nothing like it has occurred (certainly not in peace-time) in all the two hundred years we have surveyed. There is nothing extraordinary about a 7 per cent. Bank Rate; that has happened before; but in former times it was not implied by a high Bank Rate that the long-term rate would behave in this fashion. Excepting in the Aftermaths, when a great weight of long-term Debt has overhung the market, a 7 per cent. Bank Rate has been consistent with a long-term rate which has not passed outside its traditional norm of 3–3½ per cent. It is the 6 per cent. long-term rate which is the extraordinary feature of the situation to which we have come. How, on the principles which I have been elaborating, do we explain it?

Since there is not, at this time, any exceptional weight of long-term Debt (that, I think, remains true, even if we add the obligations of the Nationalized Industries and the Local Authorities to those of the Government itself), the height of the long-term rate cannot be explained save by assuming that the market's *expectations* are now of high rates: that high Bank Rates are no longer thought of as being temporary accidents, but are beginning to be regarded as normal. By putting into reverse the analysis of the state of mind of the thirties (which I gave above), we can see how that can have happened. It is partly that expectations have become more volatile; when the old assurances are gone, people project into the future whatever it is that chances to be happening in the present. Then it was monetary ease—so monetary ease was assumed to be going to last for ever; now it is monetary stringency—so we assume ourselves to be saddled with dear money for as far ahead as we care to look. If people had confidence in the restoration of the old norms, they would be unable to resist the bargains that are offered by these high rates (and consequent low prices of securities).

That is the 'psychological' explanation; but may it not be that there is something else, more rational (or somewhat more rational) behind it? As we saw, the expectation of low interest rates in the thirties need not be taken to have been irrational; is it not possible that the present state of mind can be rationalized in a corresponding way? Is it *reasonable* to expect that these high interest rates (and corresponding high money rates) are the normal thing that we have to expect for the future? I think that there are two issues here—

associated but still distinct issues—the question of inflation and the question of reserves.

If one looks at the question of inflation by itself, as we may permit ourselves to do for the moment, one may argue as follows. Prices have now been rising (at varying rates, but continuously) for many years; it is rising prices, not steady prices, which have now become normal. Against an expectation of rising prices the effects of high interest rates are much damped; if prices are confidently expected to rise at 3 per cent. per annum, an interest rate of 6 per cent. is the same as 3 per cent. in real terms. With sufficiently inflationary expectations, a 6 per cent. interest rate is not a high rate at all; it is merely normal. The rate would have to go higher still if it was to exercise any restraining effect.

One may doubt whether the authorities would be willing to risk the unemployment, and other misfortunes, which might well attend any attempt to stop inflation altogether by a really sharp application of a monetary brake; and one may yet have confidence that they will be unwilling to speed it unnecessarily by a Daltonian policy of cheap money for its own sake. So long as inflation continues, and this kind of monetary policy continues, so long (it would seem) we must expect a continuance of dear, but not ultra-dear, money; that would mean that long-term rates would go on being rather high. Only if there were a temporary shift to a policy of drastic restriction, which stopped the inflation in its tracks, would it be possible for money to become really cheap later on. If such a dénouement were really to be expected, it would be rational for the long-term rate to come down.

One can argue that way, but it has become abundantly clear that it is by no means the whole story. The most direct evidence that it is not the whole story is that a more or less parallel rise in interest has been going on, in several other countries (which have experienced very different rates of internal inflation), especially in those countries which had quite long periods of low interest rates in the past. In the United States, the long-term rate on Government bonds has risen from $2\frac{1}{2}$ per cent. at the beginning of the fifties, to 3 per cent. in 1956, to 4 per cent. after 1959, and to more than $4\frac{1}{2}$ per cent. in 1966. In the Netherlands, the corresponding rate has gone up from $3\frac{1}{4}$ per cent. in the early fifties to 5 per cent. in 1964–5. Even in Switzerland there has been a rise from 3 to 4 per cent. over the same period. At the time when the first version of this paper was written (in 1958), though it was already apparent that the problem was one of reserves, as well as of inflation, it could still be looked at as a mainly British problem. In 1966–7 that is no longer possible.

The international problem that has arisen is nevertheless in some sense a generalization of what had already appeared in the British case. One could already say, in 1958, that the dear money which had already appeared in Britain, was not in the main a non-violent anti-inflationary measure; it was mainly motivated by the desire to maintain a stable exchange. And the reason why it was difficult to maintain a stable exchange was not internal inflation (which was not then, whatever it has been since, a serious threat to sterling). What made us weak, so prone to repeated exchange crises, was lack of reserves. It was because our reserves were so low that we had to go on jabbing at the money rate in the face of temporary accidents, which with adequate reserves we could have ridden out.

When, in the thirties, we allowed the exchange to float, our reserves of gold and dollars, relative to the claims which might be made upon them, were relatively ample; but in the late fifties they had already fallen to a fraction of their size in that earlier period. That is one of the reasons why we could have a floating pound in the thirties, for it was generally true that the pound did not have to fall further (and it was known that it did not have to fall further) than the authorities were prepared to allow it to fall. Already in 1958 (and still more today) there would be no such assurance. If we were driven off $2.80, we should have to *fix* a lower parity; but we should have to defend that lower parity with all the weapons that remained to us, including high Bank Rate and (no doubt) a stiffening of exchange control. We could not avoid the necessity of high money rates by devaluing.

All that is as true, as far as Britain is concerned, in 1967 as it was in 1958; but now it is not Britain only, it is other countries also, that are short of international reserves. This, it is clear, cannot be a problem of inflation; for the shortage, though at any particular time it is felt more acutely by some countries than by others, is really quite general; and how can everyone be inflating more than everyone else? If we look back to an earlier stage of the story I have been telling in this paper, we can begin to understand what it is that has happened.

I have explained that one (at least) of the reasons for the gradual fall in the Yield on Consols which continued for so many years during the Long Peace of the nineteenth century was the expansion of credit. There was an increased (relative) supply of many sorts of credit instruments, mostly of a very reliable character; it was the expansion of this 'secondary liquidity', added to the gold base, which enabled the long-term debt to be more easily carried. What we have been seeing in these last years is a process which is of the same character, projected on to the international plane, and *put into reverse.*

In order that international credit should be usable, internationally, as 'secondary liquidity', it must be dependable. It must be freely convertible into means of international payment, at a rate of exchange which can be relied upon not to move adversely, or not to any very serious extent. During the Long Peace, sterling claims were thus dependable; they were often usable directly as international money, and they were always reliably convertible so as to be usable for the payment of debts not expressed in sterling. That position, fully attained up to 1914, has never, even in the most favourable years since that date, been fully restored. But there were many years, in the middle of the century, when an alternative 'secondary liquidity' was provided by the U.S.

dollar; not that it was ever so directly useful as a means of payment, but it was safe to hold it, since it was freely convertible into other currencies, and it very rarely happened that any other currency appreciated against it. But since the 'dollar scare' of 1958–9, not even the dollar has been regarded as quite fully secure. Though dollar balances are still employed as international liquid assets, their 'quality' is impaired; they are no longer quite 'as good as gold'. And so there is a scramble for gold which if it is to take the place of the secondary liquidity that is ceasing to be available, is in seriously short supply. That is the basic cause of the *international* rise in interest rates.

In the light of this analysis, I am much in agreement with those who look for a way out, not in terms of devaluations, either particular or general, but through the development of new and more dependable sources of international liquidity.[1] Though by devaluations the supply of gold would be increased, in terms of some (or even of many) national monetary units, the quality of such secondary liquidity as is now available would be weakened still further, and the loss might well offset, or more than offset, the gain. It is not so much that the gold base requires to be enlarged, as that the secondary liquidity, provided by claims expressed in what could still be reasonably sound currencies, should be made more secure. We have the beginnings of an international system which can reinforce dependability—in the IMF and in other forms of central banking co-operation; through them what was done, in the old days, for national monetary systems could be done, at least to some extent, internationally.

[1] I think particularly of the papers by Professor Machlup and by Professor Triffin which have appeared (and continue to appear) among the publications of the International Finance Section of Princeton University.

6

THE PURE THEORY OF PORTFOLIO
SELECTION

I

THE theory of portfolio selection is a part of the theory
of decision-making under uncertainty. It may be defined as
that part in which the chooser is taken to be operating upon
a perfect market—in the 'perfect competition' sense that the
prospect of return on a unit of money placed in a given
manner is taken to be independent of the number of units of
money that are so placed. Such a theory will not often apply
to investment in real capital (say in stocks of materials) where
the prospect of return per unit of money invested must often
depend very much upon the amount that is invested; it is by
no means universally applicable to Stock Exchange and other
financial investment, since operation on a sufficiently large
scale will affect the prospect of return on £1 by affecting the
price of the security that is purchased. It must nevertheless
have some applicability to Stock Exchange investment; but it
may be that its main importance is in being a relatively tract-
able part of uncertainty theory. Thus it is an area in which we
may try our wings, before we venture (if we dare to venture)
upon the more difficult and exciting parts of the territory.

One of the reasons why it is useful to exercise ourselves in
this area is that we can use it as a field in which to test alternative assumptions about maximand: about the nature of
the index which the chooser is supposed to be maximizing.
Some of the hypotheses which have been proposed (such as
Professor Shackle's[1]) come under suspicion at once because

---

[1] See, for instance, R. E. D. Egerton, *Investment Decisions under Uncertainty*, pp. 20–21.

of their apparent inapplicability to portfolio theory; others (as will be seen) which are unquestionably applicable, yield curious results, which may be mistaken for predictions about actual behaviour, but prove to be due to nothing more than arbitrary restrictions that have been concealed within the hypothesis. The 'general' theory, with which this paper is mainly concerned, goes a good way (it would be rash to claim that it goes the whole way) towards the avoidance of such arbitrary restrictions. Relatively to other versions, it is rather empty of predictive capacity. But that (I believe) is how it should be. Theory, of this sort, is not by itself an engine for the discovery of truth; but even by itself it can be an apparatus for the avoidance of error.

Though the portfolio selection problem has analogies with the consumer choice problem, there is one fundamental difference. The consumer buys lemonade because he likes lemonade, but the investor does not buy ICI because he likes ICI. His investment in a particular security is solely a means to an end—the attainment of the best prospect of return over his whole portfolio. Corresponding to each distribution of placings that is available to him, within the total capital to be invested, there will be a particular prospect of return. This correspondence, though it depends upon his interpretation of the evidence that is at his disposal, has nothing to do with his *choice*. There is a choice between different prospects; some may prefer one prospect and some another. The problem is to find an index, which must refer to the total prospect, which the chooser can fairly be represented as maximizing.

In order to find such an index, we must first have a way of reducing the prospect itself into formal terms. We can do this if we separate the certain and the uncertain elements in the prospect, in the manner that has been made familiar in Game Theory. Say that there are m 'eventualities',[1] any one of which may occur. Which will occur is not known, but the

---

[1] Or 'states of the world', as it is becoming common to call them. I prefer a less pompous description.

return on £1, placed in the ith security, if the jth eventuality occurs, is supposed to be known. The probability (p_i) of each of the m eventualities is also supposed to be known.[1] By this device the prospect is reduced to the regular form of a probability distribution, so that it can be manipulated in the regular manner of the theory of probability.

If a_{ij} is the return (per £ invested) on the jth security in the ith eventuality, and if x_j is the amount invested in the jth security, then $v_i = \sum a_{ij} x_j$ is the return, over the whole portfolio, in the ith eventuality, from the set of placings (x_j). The probability distribution of the v_i's is the prospect of return, over the whole portfolio, from that particular distribution of placings.

The alternative indices, which we shall be discussing, can in these terms be readily compared.

1. The simplest possible index is the mean value or mathematical expectation of the prospect, which I shall call E ($= \sum p_i v_i$). But this, as is well known (the point will be illustrated in our further work) has to be rejected, at least in the present application. An investor who proceeded on this principle would place the whole of his capital in a single security, that for which the mean value of return (per £ invested) was the highest. The trouble with this principle is that it leaves no scope for the normal (and surely rational) practice of spreading risks.

2. It was suggested, centuries ago, by Bernouilli, that in order to overcome the manifest defects of this first principle, it should be substituted by a maximization of 'expected utility'. That is to say, instead of maximizing E, the investor should be taken to be maximizing $\sum p_i \, u(v_i)$, where $u(v)$ is a *total* utility function, with the usual property of having a positive but diminishing first derivative (diminishing marginal utility). This assumption has had a great vogue in recent years; in some applications, as to the Theory of Games and to the foundations of Statistical Theory, it has without question done good service. But in the present application it

[1] See above, p. 20.

does not justify itself. For it only gives manageable results, which can be tested against experience, if we take the utility function $u(v)$ in a very simple form; and in its simplest forms it, like the first principle, gives results that are not acceptable. How it is that this happens will be demonstrated as we go on.

3. The third alternative is to look at the regular statistical parameters of the prospect, considered as a probability distribution—not just the first moment (E) but other moments also. In order to get a complete description of a complex distribution many moments may be required, and the complexity of the resulting theory would soon pass all bounds; but it turns out that the distinctions we need to make emerge sufficiently when we use a quite small number of further moments. Even to take one further moment (the variance or standard deviation) is a great gain; and many writers upon the subject[1] have considered that to be sufficient. I have myself come in the end[2] to doubt if it is quite sufficient; the results which we get from the two-moment theory need at least to be tested to see how far they stand up to the inclusion of further moments. I shall do a bit of that testing before I have done; but in most of what follows I shall confine myself to the two-moment theory.

II

A choice which has been reduced to a choice between two parameters can be represented on a two-dimensional diagram (Fig. 5). E (the mean value of return over the whole portfolio) is measured on the horizontal axis. I prefer to take S (the standard deviation) as the second parameter, since (like E) it is a sum of money, while the variance (S^2) is in units that one cannot recognize. (There are further

[1] For instance, J. Tobin, 'The Theory of Portfolio Selection', in the IEA volume, *The Theory of Interest Rates*; J. Lintner, 'Valuation of Risk Assets' (*Review Economics and Statistics*, February 1965).

[2] In my own paper 'Liquidity' (*EJ*, 1962), the method of which is largely followed here, I confined myself to the two-moment theory.

reasons, which will appear later, which indicate that S is a more convenient choice.) Since greater S is taken to be a disutility, I measure S on the vertical axis drawn *downwards*.

To every portfolio that might be selected there will correspond a point on the diagram (there may be more than one possible portfolio corresponding to the same point, but that does not matter). Portfolios that can be selected, consistently

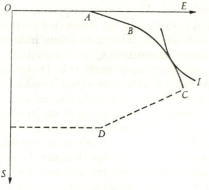

FIG. 5

with the fixed amount of investible capital, will lie within a *feasible region*, with a definite *frontier*.

If there is any security which gives an absolutely safe return (standard deviation o), to put the whole of the capital into that security is one possible choice; the return on the whole capital, put into that security, will be represented by a point on the E-axis. If there are several such securities, there will be a point on the E-axis corresponding to each; but if (as we must surely suppose) the marginal utility of E is positive, it will be only that point which lies furthest to the right which can lie upon the effective frontier. This is the point which is marked as A on the diagram. (What happens when there is no such safe investment will be considered later.)

It is clear that from A the frontier must slope downwards

to the right. For if the marginal utility of E is positive and that of S is negative, risky alternatives which fail to give a larger E than at A must be inferior to A. But there is a good deal more that can be said about the shape of the frontier.

At A the whole capital is put into the safe security; the safest way to get a slightly better return than at A (over the whole portfolio) is to put a small part of the capital into something a little more risky. But how is this 'something more risky' to be selected? One might suppose, at first sight, that a single security, of nearly the same degree of safety, would be chosen; but (if one abstracts from indivisibilities, and costs of making investments, which will be deliberately neglected in the present paper[1]) this is wrong. The safest way to get the extra E is to spread one's risks. The small part of the capital, which is put at risk, should be divided among the available securities, combining them in such proportions as will enable the additional E to be 'bought' at the expense of additional S, on terms that are as favourable as possible. These proportions, in which the 'bundle' is to be combined, are entirely dependent upon the prospects of the individual securities; they are a 'technical' matter, having nothing to do with (E, S) preferences.[2]

Then, as one moves along the frontier from A downwards, the investment in the safe security diminishes and that in the bundle increases; and the bundle (being composed of securities in fixed proportions) can of course be treated, in the usual way, as if it were a single security. Thus the portfolio has two elements, the safe security and the bundle. Let x_0 be the amount invested in the safe security and x_1 the amount invested in the bundle. Let e_0 be the mean value of the prospect of return on the safe security, and s_0 $(= 0)$ its standard deviation; e_1 $(> e_0)$ and s_1 (> 0) correspondingly for the bundle. Then

$$E = e_0 x_0 + e_1 x_1, \qquad S^2 = 0 + s_1^2 x_1^2,$$

[1] In 'The Two Triads' (above, pp. 31–34) I have investigated the consequences of introducing costs of investment.
[2] See below, p. 112.

so that $S = s_1 x_1$. The total amount to be invested is constant, so that at A

$$E = E^* = e_0(x_0 + x_1).$$

Thus $E - E^* = (e_1 - e_0)x_1$, so that

$$\frac{E - E^*}{S} = \frac{e_1 - e_0}{s_1}$$

which, in view of the perfect market assumption, is independent of x_1. Thus, so long as nothing is happening save substitution between the safe security and the bundle, there is a linear relation between E and S. All along this stretch (drawn as AB on the diagram) the frontier is a straight line.

It would, of course, have been true, in the same way, that there would have been movement along a straight line in the (E, S) diagram, when *any* bundle of securities, combined in fixed proportions, was substituted, bit by bit, for the safe security. As the proportions of securities in the bundle are varied, the slope of the line will (in general) change. There must be some set of proportions which gives a line of minimum slope, and it must be this that determines the frontier; for all the rest lie inside it. (It is not possible to move to the right of A along the E-axis, since it is the safe security with maximum return that has been taken at A.)

Now consider the point B. The whole of the capital has now been put into the bundle; nothing more can be done by the substitution that sufficed along AB. But it is still likely to be possible to find another bundle, by substitution of which for the first more E can be acquired; by the use of this the frontier can be prolonged beyond B. But since the first bundle was that by which E could be bought on most favourable terms, the second bundle must offer a less favourable substitution; thus the slope of the frontier beyond B must be steeper than over AB. And it is now no longer the case that the frontier will be linear (or even polygonal), since even a simple substitution of a second bundle for a first will give

$$S^2 = s_1^2 x_1^2 + 2r_{12} s_1 s_2 x_1 x_2 + s_2^2 x_2^2$$

(r_{12} being the correlation coefficient between the prospects of the two bundles); and this will not reduce to a linear relation between E and S. This is sufficient to show that the frontier must bend round between B and C, as drawn.

Now consider C. I show the frontier cut off at C, where E is the maximum mean value that can be got by placing the whole of the capital into any single available security, without attention to variance. The feasible region may, of course, include such points as D, at which S is higher than at C, though E is lower. But these, it is evident, cannot lie upon the effective frontier.

An investor who proceeded according to our first principle, of maximizing E without attention to S, would simply choose the position C. But if he has aversion from S, he will choose some point on the frontier ABC. We can (formally) show the position that will be chosen by confronting the frontier with s set of (E, S) indifference curves. Since the frontier (as has been shown) is necessarily convex, we have only to make the conventional assumptions about the form of these indifference curves, and we are assured that any tangency will represent a true maximum. There is no need to investigate that matter in any more complicated way.

The 'safe security', which has been a convenient expository device, can now (if we choose) be discarded. All that happens, if it is discarded, is that the linear stretch AB is removed. The safest position that can be got is to put all the capital into the safest 'bundle', which will now be represented by the point B. The feasible region can be closed (if we so wish) by a horizontal line through B.

III

The properties of the (E, S) frontier are adequately displayed for many purposes by the preceding almost non-algebraical argument. It may, however, be useful, before going further, to elaborate upon it a little.

We are supposing that the investor is maximizing a utility

function $U(E, S)$. In order that this should be done the marginal utilities of all investments that are used must be equalized, while those of investments that are not used must be less than this common value. For the marginal utility of the jth investment we have

$$U_j = U_E E_j + U_S S_j$$

(suffixes standing for partial derivatives). Since U_E and U_S occur in each U_j, we may divide through by U_E, equalizing the *marginal advantages*

$$A_j = (U_j/U_E) = E_j - WS_j,$$

where $W\ (= -U_S/U_E)$ is the marginal rate of substitution between E and S, that must be equal to the slope of our frontier.

Let e_j and s_j be the mean value and standard deviation of the unit prospects of the jth security (in accordance with previous notation); let x_j be the amount invested in the jth security; let the safe security be denoted, as before, by the suffix zero. Then

$$E = e_0 x_0 + \sum e_j x_j$$
$$S^2 = \sum s_j^2 x_j^2 + 2 \sum r_{jk} s_j s_k x_j x_k \quad (k \neq j)$$

so that

$$A_j = e_j - (W/S)s_j(s_j x_j + \sum r_{jk} s_k x_k) \quad (k \neq j),$$
$$A_0 = e_0.$$

Let K be the total capital that is to be invested, so that

$$K = x_0 + \sum x_j$$

and let M be the common value of the marginal advantages of those securities that are taken. Clearly, if $x_0 > 0$, $M = e_0$; and if $M > e_0$, $x_0 = 0$. (It is impossible that $M < e_0$, if the safe security, with constant marginal advantage equal to e_0, is available.)

For the 'risky' securities that are taken, $A_j = M$; so that

$$s_j(s_j x_j + \sum r_{jk} s_k x_k) = (e_j - M)(S/W).$$

The left-hand side of this equation is a linear function of the x's, while (S/W) is a common multiplier; thus the proportions (x_j/x_k) in which the risky securities are combined depend upon M only. Whenever $x_0 > 0$, M is constant; thus the proportions are constant; the 'bundle' (as was formerly observed) must be combined in proportions that remain unchanged so long as x_0 is positive.

If we multiply the last equation by x_j, and sum over all the 'risky' securities, the left-hand side sums to S^2, so that

$$S^2 = (\sum e_j x_j - M \sum x_j)(S/W)$$
$$= (E - e_0 x_0 - MK + Mx_0)(S/W).$$

Now it is either the case that $e_0 = M$, or $x_0 = 0$; so that *in either case*

$$S^2 = (E - MK)(S/W)$$

or $\qquad\qquad E - WS = MK.$

Since W (the marginal rate of substitution) is the slope of the frontier, this tells us that the intercept of the tangent to the frontier on the E-axis is equal to MK. This is equal to $e_0 K \ (= E^*)$ so long as $x_0 > 0$—which establishes the linearity of the 'AB' stretch; while it is clear that M will rise as risk-aversion diminishes, so that the curved part of the frontier must be convex outwards, as drawn.

All this is valid whatever are the intercorrelations between the prospects of the risky securities. In the particular case where the prospects are independent, so that all $r_{jk} = 0$, we can go rather further.

For the equilibrium equation, for any risky security that is positively held, will then reduce to

$$s^2 x_j = (e_j - M)(S/W)$$

and it is at once apparent that the condition for such a security to be admissible into the portfolio is simply that its $e_j > M$. Thus if $M = e_0$, all securities will be taken that have an $e_j > e_0$. When $M > e_0$, securities with $e_j < M$ are cut out; the optimal position is got by spreading widely over such securities as remain. (This implies, of course, as throughout this paper, that there are no costs of investment and disinvestment.)

This rule about spreading is the only part of the theory which depends upon an absence of intercorrelation. It becomes obvious at once that if there is intercorrelation, it may not hold. For consider the simplest case, in which there are just two risky securities that have intercorrelated prospects. Call them 1 and 2. Then for these securities, we have equilibrium equations—I simplify by writing h_j for $(e_j - M)/s^2$

$$s_1 x_1 + rs_2 x_2 = h_1(S/W)$$
$$rs_1 x_1 + s_2 x_2 = h_2(S/W)$$

which solve to

$$(1-r^2)s_1 x_1 = (h_1 - rh_2)(S/W)$$
$$(1-r^2)s_2 x_2 = (h_2 - rh_1)(S/W).$$

The consequences of this solution may be summarized in words as follows, if we allow ourselves to give a name to h. Suppose we call it the *attractiveness* of the security. Let

$$h_1 > h_2.$$

If $r > 0$, the less attractive security will be taken, in conjunction with the first, only if $r < h_2/h_1$. Highly correlated securities will both be taken only if they are nearly equally attractive. If $r < 0$, both will be taken if they both have positive attractiveness. But it then becomes possible that a security may be taken, even if it has negative attractiveness, for its employment will tend to offset the risk on the other. Thus the second security may be taken, even if h_2 is negative, when

$$(-r)h_1 > -h_2$$

(if this condition is satisfied, the other necessarily follows).

Conditions of this sort will determine the selection of risky securities that are to be selected, out of the whole number available. It does not seem worth while to pursue this principle of selection further.

IV

Let us return to our diagram (Fig. 5). The frontier, as drawn, implies that the total sum to be invested (K) is given; but the *shape* of the frontier depends upon the prospects of return of the individual securities. If these prospects remained unchanged, but the sum to be invested increased, the frontier would shift, but it would shift in a determinate way. There is a pattern of investment corresponding to each point on the frontier, in the sense of a set of proportions in which the capital is divided among the securities. If this pattern remained unchanged, while capital increased by so much per cent., both E and S would be increased by that same percentage so the frontier would be *magnified*, expanding uniformly along vectors through the origin. The new point of equilibrium would be found at the point where the 'magnified' frontier touched one of the family of indifference curves.

If one just draws one's indifference curves freehand, merely keeping them concave upwards in the usual manner, it is very easy to draw them so that they show a shift to the left along the frontier as capital increases—implying a tendency for the investor to play safer as he gets richer. But a procedure of this kind is of course completely inconclusive. There is no apparent reason why the successive indifference curves should not be related to one another as the successive frontier curves are related—in the way that the successive contour lines of a constant returns to scale production function are related—one being derived from another by magnification along vectors through the origin. A system of indifference curves, so constructed, will be perfectly well behaved. If the indifference map was of this form, magnification would not change proportions; so the proportions in which the portfolio was divided among securities would be independent of its size. There seems to be in general no reason why we should not take this to be the standard case: a case from which there might be divergence, in practical experience, in either direction. A shift, if it occurred, would be a pure scale effect (like the income effect of static demand theory); one does not expect that there will be any theoretical reason why scale effects should go in any particular direction.

That is the negative (but emancipating) conclusion which seems to emerge from the (E, S) approach to portfolio theory; if one had adopted a Bernouillian approach one might have concluded otherwise. For suppose that we do think of the investor as maximizing $\sum p_i u(v_i)$; and, for convenience in handling, suppose that we take the utility function in the simplest form that is possible, namely that in which the marginal utility 'curves' are downward-sloping straight lines. The *total* utility $u(v_i)$ can then be written as

$$a + bv_i - \tfrac{1}{2}cv_i^2$$

(a, b, c being positive constants). If one takes this form of function, expected utility is expressible in terms of E and S. For

$$\sum p_i(a + bv_i - \tfrac{1}{2}cv_i^2)$$
$$= a \sum p_i + b \sum p_i v_i - \tfrac{1}{2}c \sum p_i v_i^2$$
$$= a + bE - \tfrac{1}{2}c(E^2 + S^2).$$

If this expression was put equal to a constant, we should get the equation of one of our (E, S) indifference curves. But what equation is it? It is the equation of a circle. The successive indifference curves are a family of concentric circles. This is a very special kind of indifference map; it is no wonder that it has peculiar properties.

Suppose one does take this form, and calculates the marginal rate of substitution between E and S. We get

$$W = (-U_S/U_E) = cS/(b - cE)$$

so that $(b/c) = E + (S/W)$. It follows from this equation that if W is constant (when K varies) E and S must move in opposite directions. Now suppose that we begin from a position on the linear stretch AB, so the marginal rate of substitution has to equal the *fixed* slope of the line AB. If there is a small increase in capital, the line AB will move parallel to itself; its slope will be unchanged. Continuity will require that the point of equilibrium remains on the linear stretch. On this stretch, $E - WS = e_0 K$. Taking this equation in conjunction with the other, it is clear that when K rises, E will rise, but S *must fall*. The proportion of capital that is put into the safe security must therefore increase.

Starting from the Bernouillian assumption, it is easy to arrive at a conclusion of this kind. But it is really no more than a property of concentric circles; it has nothing to do with economics.[1]

This, however, is not the only way in which one may be led into a similar paradox. There is another way; though it is no less of a mare's nest, it is of somewhat greater economic interest.

Suppose that the return on the safe security is actually zero. The linear part of the frontier will then pass through the origin. On magnification, accordingly, this part of the frontier will not be moved; all that will happen is that it is extended in length. It must therefore happen that if the initial equilibrium was on the stretch AB, and the indifference curves have not shifted, the point of equilibrium will not shift as a result of the magnification. E and S will both be unaffected; and this can happen only if the *whole* of the additional capital is put into the safe security. It is not merely that the investor will have a bias in favour of increased safety on becoming wealthier; he cannot be induced to put *any more* into risky securities by being made better off.

This is obvious nonsense; yet it has apparently arisen even within the (E, S) theory. What is it that has happened? It is tempting to identify the safe security, in this application, with Keynesian 'money'—the security that yields no interest. If there is any speculative demand for money, the above analysis (so it seems at first sight) ought to apply. But in

---

[1] If one introduces further positive powers, making one's utility function $u = a + bv - (\frac{1}{2})cv^2 + (\frac{1}{6})dv^3 - \ldots$, one will still find that one has got a quite *special* form of utility function when it is expressed in terms of moments. If one introduces negative powers (which might be expected to avoid the slide towards safety), the determination of the portfolio equilibrium itself becomes extremely difficult.

fact it does not fit. For Keynesian money is not held for the sake of its yield—its zero yield—it is held for its capital value. Thus if we are to interpret the safe security as Keynesian money, we must not identify its *yield* with the *return*, the prospect of which is to be optimized. We must look at the whole capital value of the portfolio, as it is expected to be at some future date: not even interest *plus* capital gain, but interest *plus* capital gain *plus* initial capital value. On this interpretation, the return on money is not zero, but unity. So the point *A* will not coincide with the origin, and can move to the right on magnification. There is then, as we have seen, no reason why there should be a shift to safety when capital increases.[1]

If we do not adopt this interpretation, but insist that the 'income yield' on the portfolio is the thing to be optimized, a holding of 'money' must be considered to be motivated by the use that the investor expects (or hopes) to make of it in the future, by moving into some income-yielding security on more favourable terms than is possible at the present. In this more forward-looking sense the return on money is not zero; nor is it, in the sense required by the theory, a perfectly safe security. Again, therefore, the paradox does not hold.

V

That concludes what I shall say about (*E*, *S*) theory. It has come off reasonably well against the rivals so far considered, but one is left with an obstinate feeling that it does not go far enough. Why should the first and second moments of the

---

[1] I believe it is this which is the source of the fallacy in the famous Domar–Musgrave paper, 'Proportional Income Taxation and Risk-taking' (*QJE*, 1944, reprinted in *Readings in the Theory of Taxation*). Their contention that the effect of a proportional tax with perfect loss-offset is to encourage risk-taking is equivalent to that which is here under consideration. For if one looks solely at yield, the effect of such a tax, on an investor who is operating in a perfect market, is exactly the same as the effect of a capital levy; so that the Domar–Musgrave proposition comes to the same thing as saying that an increase in capital leads to 'playing for safety'. In order that the proposition should hold, there must be some security which is taken and which offers *certainty* of a *zero* return.

probability distribution be all that we must take into account? It will make things much harder if we try to go further; but there are some tiresome issues which we shall not clear up unless we attempt to do so.

Take the following very simple example. There is one portfolio which offers a 90 per cent. chance of an outcome of 4, and a 10 per cent. chance of an outcome of 14; the mean value of the prospect is 5, and the standard deviation is 3. There is another which offers a 90 per cent. chance of 6 and 10 per cent. chance of -4; the mean value is again 5, and the standard deviation again 3. It is implied in (E, S) theory that the investor would be indifferent between these two outcomes, which are skewed in opposite ways. But it is not by any means obvious that we are justified in assuming that he would be indifferent, though it is not easy to say straight off which would be preferred. Though the two prospects are equally *uncertain*, common parlance would surely say that one was more *risky* than the other.

In order to distinguish between prospects such as these, we have to introduce a third parameter. In order to keep it as a sum of money, like the others, we will have to make it the cube root of the third moment about the mean. (There are snags about this, but it seems on the whole to be the best course.) Call this parameter Q.

Excepting for the case in which the whole capital is put into the safe security, S is necessarily positive; E (as we have seen) can be taken to be positive; but what about the sign of Q? There is in principle no reason why Q should not take either sign, for a probability distribution can be skewed either way; and this, we shall find, is a considerable complication. Yet it is a question how far we should allow ourselves to be troubled by it. When we speak of the problem that is being here considered as a problem of risk-bearing, we are surely making the tacit assumption that most, at least, of the investments that are in question have prospects that are negatively skewed. Thus it seems reasonable to begin with the (relatively simple) theory which will suffice for negative skewness. How far it can be extended to deal with positive skewness, of the prospects of single investments on the one hand, and of the prospect of the whole portfolio on the other, we can see later.

Over the range in which Q is negative, it seems safe to say that its marginal utility will be positive. For the *risk* that we associate with a negative Q is surely the kind of risk which people are normally desirous of avoiding—by such devices as insurance. When he insures, the individual is (usually) giving up something in mean value (E) in order to get an increase in Q (a reduction in $-Q$). In order that it should be rational to do this, the marginal utility of Q must be positive.

We can further assure ourselves, in the case of a cautious investor, that his marginal utility of Q should be *diminishing*. He will be particularly concerned to avoid a *large* negative Q; but when negative skewness becomes small, the avoidance of it is a less important matter. That this does imply a diminishing marginal utility may be seen if we consider that such an investor is also likely to avoid a large positive skewness. For if E and S are given, a large positive Q implies the payment of a high price (in terms of the return that he is most likely to get) in order that he should win a big prize in some relatively improbable eventuality. Our cautious investor will surely abhor such 'speculation'. At that point his marginal utility of Q will surely have become negative. (We see at once how it is that such an investor may find it hard to choose between the two prospects which we took for our simple arithmetical illustration, since one of them is skewed 'too much' one way, and the other is skewed 'too much' the other.)

In the light of these considerations, it seems reasonable to begin by making the assumptions: (1) that the prospects of the individual risky investments are negatively skewed, so that the prospect of the whole portfolio, if any of any risky investment is taken, will be negatively skewed; and (2) that the marginal utility of Q is positive, but diminishes as Q increases, falling to zero when $Q = 0$, or thereabouts. If these assumptions can be made, the (E, S, Q) theory is quite straightforward; it is a natural generalization of the (E, S) theory formerly considered.

For the (E, S, Q) indifference surfaces will be perfectly well-behaved; while the frontier of the feasible region can be found, in the same manner as formerly, by maximizing E, minimizing S, and maximizing Q, against given values of

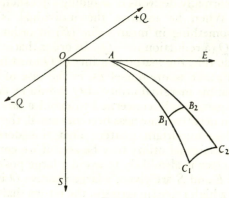

Fig. 6

the other parameters. Just as (with a finite number of available securities) the (E, S) frontier was bounded—extending from A (or B) to C, on Fig. 5, but no further in either direction—so the (E, S, Q) frontier will be bounded. It will take the form of a curvilinear triangle, such as $A C_1 C_2$ (Fig. 6) if there is a safe security; if there is not, it will be a quadrilateral $(B_1 B_2 C_2 C_1)$ similarly extended over a curved surface. The point of equilibrium is the point of this triangle (or quadrilateral) which lies on the highest indifference surface.

It is still the case that when the capital to be invested increases, the new frontier will be derived from the old by magnification along vectors through the origin. (This depends, of course, upon our 'cube root' definition of Q.) How the point of equilibrium moves depends on the way in which successive indifference surfaces are related to one another. Here again, however, there is no reason why the successive surfaces should not be related to one another by simple magnification; so, once again, there is no reason why the additional capital should not be divided between safe and risky securities (in the Q as well as in the S sense, which we can here distinguish) in the same proportions as the old. The effect of an increase in capital is just the usual scale effect.

VI

This argument about scale does not depend upon the convexity of the frontier surface; for even without such convexity there can still be an equilibrium, which will shift in the same way when the capital changes. It is true that the equilibrium must then lie upon the boundary of the triangle (or quadrilateral); but that makes no difference. For even if the surface is convex, it is still quite possible that the equilibrium may lie upon the boundary.

There is nevertheless every reason to suppose—once the particular assumptions about negativity of skewness that were made in the last section are granted—that the surface will have the convexity property, so that it bends the 'regular' way. This can be checked up if we use the alternative approach by 'marginal advantage' that was employed in section III above. If we are simply concerned with the division of a portfolio between two investments (and that will suffice for the present purpose) the point can be put on a diagram.[1]

We have now, for the marginal utility of the jth investment,

$$U_j = U_E E_j + U_S S_j + U_Q Q_j$$

so that the marginal advantage

$$A_j = E_j - WS_j + ZQ_j \quad \text{(putting } Z \text{ for } U_Q/U_E\text{)}.$$

[1] For fuller discussion of this diagram see 'The Two Triads' (above, pp. 21–26).

If the prospects of the securities are independent (we may here confine ourselves to the case of independence), this expands to

$$A_j = e_j - (W/S)s_j^2\, x_j + (Z/Q^2)q_j^3\, x_j^2.$$

At the point of equilibrium, it will be the same W, S, Z, and Q that figure in the marginal advantages of each investment, so that when we are comparing marginal advantages, all of these may be treated as constants, and A_j becomes a function of x_j only. In the (E, S) theory (which is the special case of the present where $Z = 0$), the marginal advantage *curve* can evidently be drawn out, on this principle, as a downward-sloping straight line. (The marginal advantage curve of the safe security will, then as now, be a horizontal line.) If we have just two investments, among which a given capital (OK) is to be divided, the division can be shown by starting one marginal advantage from a vertical axis above O, and the other from a vertical axis above K, and showing the equilibrium at their intersection.[1]

Skewness, we see, introduces a quadratic term into the expression for the marginal advantage; but if (as we have been hitherto supposing) Z is positive and q is negative, this quadratic term is definitely negative. The marginal advantage curve is no longer linear, but it is bent inwards, in the manner that is shown on the curves that are drawn in Fig. 7. His aversion from 'risk' makes the investor less willing to add to investments that are risky in this sense; and that is as it should be. But there is no reason why the equilibrium should be any less 'stable' in this case than in the linear (E, S) case.[2]

Nevertheless, having got this apparatus, it is natural to use it in order to inquire what will happen if *one* of the investments has a skewness that goes the other way. If q is positive (Z being still positive), the quadratic term will be positive, and the divergence from linearity will be in the opposite direction.

[1] As in Figs. 1–3, pp. 25–26.
[2] The curve will have a maximum at a point where x_j is negative.

Now it is inevitable that a curve of the second degree, having these signs for its coefficients, will eventually turn upwards, and will then continue to rise *ad infinitum*. This does not make it impossible that there should be a stable equilibrium, in which the portfolio is divided between one 'risky' and one 'speculative' security. One way in which this might happen is

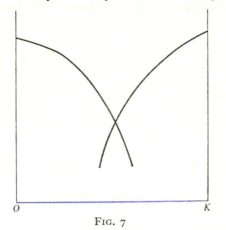

FIG. 7

shown in Fig. 8. It must, however, be expected that the speculative security (if it exists) will have a strong tendency to draw investment to itself, for once the rising part of its curve can become effective, it will be extremely powerful.

That is so, if the things that have so far been considered are all that is to be taken into account. There remain, however, at least two further possibilities. It will first be noticed that by shifting the distribution of his portfolio in the 'specula-tive' direction, the investor may be changing the sign of Q (over his whole portfolio). If he is not himself speculatively inclined, he may well be averse from a positive Q; so that his Z (or it may be better to say his Z/Q^2) will become negative. Even before that happens, it will fall to zero, so that the up-ward turn of the marginal advantage curve (which has caused the trouble) will disappear. That is one way in which it may be rational to combine 'speculative' with 'risky' investments; but though this may happen, the combination of the two, so that one 'offsets' the other—which is what this is—does not look a very plausible policy.

And surely there is a reason for that. The combination of investments, so that one offsets the skewness of the other, is a different kind of combination from that which the (E, S)

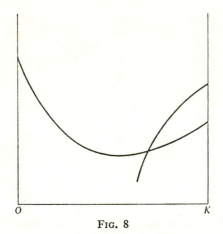

FIG. 8

theory could already deal with: the combination of investments for the *spreading* of risks. Combination with the one motive is very likely to get in the way of combination for the other. Now it may indeed be said that this point is already allowed for, by the term of the first degree in A_j; but one has a feeling that it may not be allowed for sufficiently. Do we here have a reason why even the three-moment theory may not go far enough, so that there is perfectly rational behaviour which can only be fitted in by introducing still higher moments? It is, of course, evident, as soon as a fourth moment is introduced (with the negative marginal utility which should plausibly be attached to it) that the marginal advantage curve, even of a speculative investment—a cubic curve, it would now have to be—would turn downwards in the end.[1]

There is no reason in principle, on the approach adopted in this paper, why we should not go as far as that, if it is necessary to do so. But I hope I have shown that for most purposes it is not necessary.

---

[1] The marginal advantage curve will then be 'serpentining', like the marginal utility curve in the famous Friedman–Savage article 'Utility Analysis of Choices involving Risk' (*JPE*, 1948, reprinted in AEA *Readings in Price Theory*). One must accept their demonstration that combination of speculative and risky investments is only possible, on the Bernouillian hypothesis, if one admits a range of increasing marginal utility. Nevertheless, as shown here, the Bernouillian hypothesis greatly limits the range of (E,S) or (E,S,Q) utility functions that are admissible. If one widens the range, merely insisting that the utility function must be well-behaved in the 'moment' field, one can get the 'serpentining', that is admittedly necessary, simply by introducing a sufficient number of moments.

7

MR. KEYNES AND THE 'CLASSICS'[1]
(1937)

I

IT will be admitted by the least charitable reader that the entertainment value of Mr. Keynes's *General Theory of Employment* is considerably enhanced by its satiric aspect. But it is also clear that many readers have been left very bewildered by this Dunciad. Even if they are convinced by Mr. Keynes's arguments and humbly acknowledge themselves to have been 'classical economists' in the past, they find it hard to remember that they believed in their unregenerate days the things Mr. Keynes says they believed. And there are no doubt others who find their historic doubts a stumbling block, which prevents them from getting as much illumination from the positive theory as they might otherwise have got.

One of the main reasons for this situation is undoubtedly to be found in the fact that Mr. Keynes takes as typical of 'Classical economics' the later writings of Professor Pigou, particularly *The Theory of Unemployment*. Now *The Theory of Unemployment* is a fairly new book, and an exceedingly difficult book; so that it is safe to say that it has not yet made much impression on the ordinary teaching of economics. To most people its doctrines seem quite as strange and novel as the doctrines of Mr. Keynes himself; so that to be told that he has believed these things himself leaves the ordinary economist quite bewildered.

[1] Based on a paper which was read at the Oxford meeting of the Econometric Society (September 1936) and which called forth an interesting discussion. This paper was modified subsequently, partly in the light of that discussion, and partly as a result of further discussion in Cambridge, and appeared in *Econometrica*, vol. v, no. 2, April 1937, from which it is here reproduced.

For example, Professor Pigou's theory runs, to a quite amazing extent, in real terms. Not only is his theory a theory of real wages and unemployment; but numbers of problems which anyone else would have preferred to investigate in money terms are investigated by Professor Pigou in terms of 'wage-goods'. The ordinary classical economist has no part in this *tour de force*.

But if, on behalf of the ordinary classical economist, we declare that he would have preferred to investigate many of those problems in money terms, Mr. Keynes will reply that there is no classical theory of money wages and employment. It is quite true that such a theory cannot easily be found in the textbooks. But this is only because most of the textbooks were written at a time when general changes in money wages in a closed system did not present an important problem. There can be little doubt that most economists have thought that they had a pretty fair idea of what the relation between money wages and employment actually was.

In these circumstances, it seems worth while to try to construct a typical 'classical' theory, built on an earlier and cruder model than Professor Pigou's. If we can construct such a theory, and show that it does give results which have in fact been commonly taken for granted, but which do not agree with Mr. Keynes's conclusions, then we shall at last have a satisfactory basis of comparison. We may hope to be able to isolate Mr. Keynes's innovations, and so to discover what are the real issues in dispute.

Since our purpose is comparison, I shall try to set out my typical classical theory in a form similar to that in which Mr. Keynes sets out his own theory; and I shall leave out of account all secondary complications which do not bear closely upon this special question in hand. Thus I assume that I am dealing with a short period in which the quantity of physical equipment of all kinds available can be taken as fixed. I assume homogeneous labour. I assume further that depreciation can be neglected, so that the output of investment goods corresponds to new investment. This is a dangerous simplification, but the important issues raised by Mr. Keynes in his chapter on user cost are irrelevant for our purposes.

Let us begin by assuming that w, the rate of money wages per head, can be taken as given.

Let x, y be the outputs of investment goods and consumption goods respectively, and N_x, N_y be the numbers of men employed in producing them. Since the amount of physical equipment specialized to each industry is given, $x = f_x(N_x)$ and $y = f_y(N_y)$, where f_x, f_y are *given* functions.

Let M be the *given* quantity of money.

It is desired to determine N_x and N_y.

First, the price-level of investment goods = their marginal cost = $w(dN_x/dx)$. And the price-level of consumption goods = their marginal cost = $w(dN_y/dy)$.

Income earned in investment trades (value of investment, or simply Investment) = $wx(dN_x/dx)$. Call this I_x.

Income earned in consumption trades = $wy(dN_y/dy)$.

Total Income = $wx(dN_x/dx)+wy(dN_y/dy)$. Call this I.

I_x is therefore a given function of N_x, I of N_x and N_y. Once I and I_x are determined, N_x and N_y can be determined.

Now let us assume the 'Cambridge Quantity Equation'— that there is some definite relation between Income and the demand for money. Then, approximately, and apart from the fact that the demand for money may depend not only upon total Income, but also upon its distribution between people with relatively large and relatively small demands for balances, we can write

$$M = kI.$$

As soon as k is given, total Income is therefore determined.

In order to determine I_x, we need two equations. One tells us that the amount of investment (looked at as demand for capital) depends upon the rate of interest:

$$I_x = C(i).$$

This is what becomes the marginal-efficiency-of-capital schedule in Mr. Keynes's work.

Further, Investment = Saving. And saving depends upon the rate of interest and, if you like, Income. $\therefore I_x = S(i, I)$. (Since, however, Income is already determined, we do not need to bother about inserting Income here unless we choose.)

Taking them as a system, however, we have three fundamental equations,

$$M = kI, \quad I_x = C(i), \quad I_x = S(i, I),$$

to determine three unknowns, I, I_x, i. As we have found earlier, N_x and N_y can be determined from I and I_x. Total employment, $N_x + N_y$, is therefore determined.

Let us consider some properties of this system. If follows directly from the first equation that as soon as k and M are given, I is completely determined; that is to say, total income depends directly upon the quantity of money. Total employment, however, is not necessarily determined at once from income, since it will usually depend to some extent upon the proportion of income saved, and thus upon the way production is divided between investment and consumption-goods trades. (If it so happened that the elasticities of supply were the same in each of these trades, then a shifting of demand between them would produce compensating movements in N_x and N_y, and consequently no change in total employment.)

An increase in the inducement to invest (i.e., a rightward movement of the schedule of the marginal efficiency of capital, which we have written as $C(i)$) will tend to raise the rate of interest, and so to affect saving. If the amount of saving rises, the amount of investment will rise too; labour will be employed more in the investment trades, less in the consumption trades; this will increase total employment if the elasticity of supply in the investment trades is greater than that in the consumption-goods trades—diminish it if vice versa.

An increase in the supply of money will necessarily raise total income, for people will increase their spending and lending until incomes have risen sufficiently to restore k to its former level. The rise in income will tend to increase employment, both in making consumption goods and in making investment goods. The total effect on employment depends upon the ratio between the expansions of these industries; and that depends upon the proportion of their increased incomes which people desire to save, which also governs the rate of interest.

So far we have assumed the rate of money wages to be given; but so long as we assume that k is independent of the level of wages, there is no difficulty about this problem either. A rise in the rate of money wages will necessarily diminish employment and raise real wages. For an unchanged money income cannot continue to buy an unchanged quantity of goods at a higher price-level; and, unless the price-level rises, the prices of goods will not cover their marginal costs. There must therefore be a fall in employment; as employment falls, marginal costs in terms of labour will diminish and therefore real wages rise. (Since a change in money wages is always accompanied by a change in real wages in the same direction, if not in the same proportion, no harm will be done, and some advantage will perhaps be secured, if one prefers to work in terms of real wages. Naturally most 'classical economists' have taken this line.)

I think it will be agreed that we have here a quite reasonably consistent theory, and a theory which is also consistent with the pronouncements of a recognizable group of economists. Admittedly it follows from this theory that you may be able to increase employment by direct inflation; but whether or not you decide to favour that policy still depends upon your judgement about the probable reaction on wages, and also—in a national area—upon your views about the international standard.

Historically, this theory descends from Ricardo, though it is not actually Ricardian; it is probably more or less the theory that was held by Marshall. But with Marshall it was already beginning to be qualified in important ways; his successors have qualified it still further. What Mr. Keynes has done is to lay enormous emphasis on the qualifications, so that they almost blot out the original theory. Let us follow out this process of development.

II

When a theory like the 'classical' theory we have just described is applied to the analysis of industrial fluctuations, it gets into difficulties in several ways. It is evident that total money income experiences great variations in the course of a trade cycle, and the classical theory can only explain these by variations in M or in k, or, as a third and last alternative, by changes in distribution.

(1) Variation in M is simplest and most obvious, and has been relied on to a large extent. But the variations in M that are traceable during a trade cycle are variations that take place through the banks—they are variations in bank loans; if we are to rely on them it is urgently necessary for us to explain the connexion between the supply of bank money and the rate of interest. This can be done roughly by thinking of banks as persons who are strongly inclined to pass on money by lending rather than spending it. Their action therefore tends at first to lower interest rates, and only afterwards, when the money passes into the hands of spenders, to raise prices and incomes. 'The new currency, or the increase of currency, goes, not to private persons, but to the banking centres; and therefore, it increases the willingness of lenders to lend in the first instance, and lowers the rate of discount. But it afterwards raises prices; and therefore it tends to increase discount.'[1] This is superficially satisfactory; but if we endeavoured to give a more precise account of this process we should soon get into difficulties. What determines the amount of money needed to produce a given fall in the rate of interest? What determines the length of time for which the low rate will last? These are not easy questions to answer.

(2) In so far as we rely upon changes in k, we can also do

[1] Marshall, *Money, Credit, and Commerce*, p. 257.

well enough up to a point. Changes in k can be related to changes in confidence, and it is realistic to hold that the rising prices of a boom occur because optimism encourages a reduction in balances; the falling prices of a slump because pessimism and uncertainty dictate an increase. But as soon as we take this step it becomes natural to ask whether k has not abdicated its status as an independent variable, and has not become liable to be influenced by others among the variables in our fundamental equations.

(3) This last consideration is powerfully supported by another, of more purely theoretical character. On grounds of pure value theory, it is evident that the direct sacrifice made by a person who holds a stock of money is a sacrifice of interest; and it is hard to believe that the marginal principle does not operate at all in this field. As Lavington put it:

> The quantity of resources which (an individual) holds in the form of money will be such that the unit of money which is just and only just worth while holding in this form yields him a return of convenience and security equal to the yield of satisfaction derived from the marginal unit spent on consumables, and equal also to the net rate of interest.[1]

The demand for money depends upon the rate of interest! The stage is set for Mr. Keynes.

As against the three equations of the classical theory,

$$M = kI, \quad I_x = C(i), \quad I_x = S(i, I),$$

Mr. Keynes begins with three equations,

$$M = L(i), \quad I_x = C(i), \quad I_x = S(I).$$

These differ from the classical equations in two ways. On the one hand, the demand for money is conceived as depending upon the rate of interest (Liquidity Preference). On the other hand, any possible influence of the rate of interest on the amount saved out of a given income is neglected. Although

[1] Lavington, *English Capital Market*, 1921, p. 30. See also Pigou, 'The Exchange-value of Legal-tender Money', in *Essays in Applied Economics*, 1922, pp. 179–81.

it means that the third equation becomes the multiplier equation, which performs such queer tricks, nevertheless this second amendment is a mere simplification, and ultimately insignificant.[1] It is the liquidity preference doctrine which is vital.

For it is now the rate of interest, not income, which is determined by the quantity of money. The rate of interest set against the schedule of the marginal efficiency of capital determines the value of investment; that determines income by the multiplier. Then the volume of employment (at given wage-rates) is determined by the value of investment and of income which is not saved but spent upon consumption goods.

It is this system of equations which yields the startling conclusion, that an increase in the inducement to invest, or in the propensity to consume, will not tend to raise the rate of interest, but only to increase employment. In spite of this, however, and in spite of the fact that quite a large part of the argument runs in terms of this system, and this system alone, *it is not the General Theory*. We may call it, if we like, Mr. Keynes's *special theory*. The General Theory is something appreciably more orthodox.

Like Lavington and Professor Pigou, Mr. Keynes does not in the end believe that the demand for money can be determined by one variable alone—not even the rate of interest. He lays more stress on it than they did, but neither for him nor for them can it be the only variable to be considered. The dependence of the demand for money on interest does not, in the end, do more than qualify the old

[1] This can be readily seen if we consider the equations

$$M = kI, \quad I_x = C(i), \quad I_x = S(I),$$

which embody Mr. Keynes's second amendment without his first. The third equation is already the multiplier equation, but the multiplier is shorn of his wings. For since I still depends only on M, I_x now depends only on M, and it is impossible to increase investment without increasing the willingness to save or the quantity of money. The system thus generated is therefore identical with that which, a few years ago, used to be called the 'Treasury View'. But Liquidity Preference transports us from the 'Treasury View' to the 'General Theory of Employment'.

dependence on income. However much stress we lay upon the 'speculative motive', the 'transactions' motive must always come in as well.

Consequently we have for the General Theory

$$M = L(I, i), \quad I_x = C(i), \quad I_x = S(I).$$

With this revision, Mr. Keynes takes a big step back to Marshallian orthodoxy, and his theory becomes hard to distinguish from the revised and qualified Marshallian theories, which, as we have seen, are not new. Is there really any difference between them, or is the whole thing a sham fight? Let us have recourse to a diagram (Fig. 9).

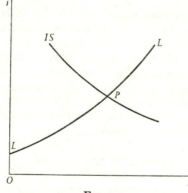

FIG. 9

Against a given quantity of money, the first equation, $M = L(I, i)$, gives us a relation between Income (I) and the rate of interest (i). This can be drawn out as a curve (LL) which will slope upwards, since an increase in income tends to raise the demand for money, and an increase in the rate of interest tends to lower it. Further, the second two equations taken together give us another relation between Income and interest. (The marginal-efficiency-of-capital schedule determines the value of investment at any given rate of interest, and the multiplier tells us what level of income will be necessary to make savings equal to that value of investment.) The curve *IS* can therefore be drawn showing the relation between Income and interest which must be maintained in order to make saving equal to investment.

Income and the rate of interest are now determined together at *P*, the point of intersection of the curves *LL* and *IS*. They are determined together; just as price and output are determined together in the modern theory of demand and supply. Indeed, Mr. Keynes's innovation is closely parallel, in this respect, to the innovation of the marginalists. The quantity theory tries to determine income without interest, just as the labour theory of value tried to determine price without output; each has to give place to a theory recognizing a higher degree of interdependence.

III

But if this is the real 'General Theory', how does Mr. Keynes come to make his remarks about an increase in the inducement to invest not raising the rate of interest? It would appear from our diagram that a rise in the marginal-efficiency-of-capital schedule must raise the curve *IS*; and, therefore, although it will raise Income and employment, it will also raise the rate of interest.

This brings us to what, from many points of view, is the most important thing in Mr. Keynes's book. It is not only possible to show that a given supply of money determines a certain relation between Income and interest (which we have expressed by the curve *LL*); it is also possible to say something about the shape of the curve. It will probably tend to be nearly horizontal on the left, and nearly vertical on the right. This is because there is (1) some minimum below which the rate of interest is unlikely to go, and (though Mr. Keynes does not stress this) there is (2) a maximum to the level of income which can possibly be financed with a given amount of money. If we like we can think of the curve as approaching these limits asymptotically (Fig. 10).

Therefore, if the curve *IS* lies well to the right (either because of a strong inducement to invest or a strong propensity to consume), *P* will lie upon that part of the curve which is decidedly upward sloping, and the classical theory will be a good approximation, needing no more than the qualification which it has in fact received at the hands of the later Marshallians. An increase in the inducement to invest will raise the rate of interest, as in the classical theory, but it

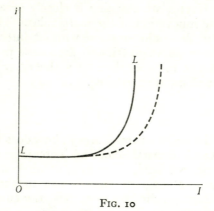

Fig. 10

will also have some subsidiary effect in raising income, and therefore employment as well. (Mr. Keynes in 1936 is not the first Cambridge economist to have a temperate faith in Public Works.) But if the point *P* lies to the left of the *LL* curve, then the *special* form of Mr. Keynes's theory becomes valid. A rise in the schedule of the marginal efficiency of capital only increases employment, and does not raise the rate of interest at all. We are completely out of touch with the classical world.

The demonstration of this minimum is thus of central importance. It is so important that I shall venture to paraphrase the proof, setting it out in a rather different way from that adopted by Mr. Keynes.[1]

[1] Keynes, *General Theory*, pp. 201–2.

If the costs of holding money can be neglected, it will always be profitable to hold money rather than lend it out, if the rate of interest is not greater than zero. Consequently the rate of interest must always be positive. In an extreme case, the shortest short-term rate may perhaps be nearly zero. But if so, the long-term rate must lie above it, for the long rate has to allow for the risk that the short rate may rise during the currency of the loan, and it should be observed that the short rate can only rise, it cannot fall.[1] This does not only mean that the long rate must be a sort of average of the probable short rates over its duration, and that this average must lie above the current short rate. There is also the more important risk to be considered, that the lender on long term may desire to have cash before the agreed date of repayment, and then, if the short rate has risen meanwhile, he may be involved in a substantial capital loss. It is this last risk which provides Mr. Keynes's 'speculative motive' and which ensures that the rate for loans of indefinite duration (which he always has in mind as *the* rate of interest) cannot fall very near zero.[2]

It should be observed that this minimum to the rate of interest applies not only to one curve *LL* (drawn to correspond to a particular quantity of money) but to any such curve. If the supply of money is increased, the curve *LL*

[1] It is just conceivable that people might become so used to the idea of very low short rates that they would not be much impressed by this risk; but it is very unlikely. For the short rate may rise, either because trade improves, and income expands; or because trade gets worse, and the desire for liquidity increases. I doubt whether a monetary system so elastic as to rule out both of these possibilities is really thinkable.

[2] Nevertheless something more than the 'speculative motive' is needed to account for the system of interest rates. The shortest of all short rates must equal the relative valuation, at the margin, of money and such a bill; and the bill stands at a discount mainly because of the 'convenience and security' of holding money—the inconvenience which may possibly be caused by not having cash immediately available. It is the chance that you may want to discount the bill which matters, not the chance that you will then have to discount it on unfavourable terms. The 'precautionary motive', not the 'speculative motive', is here dominant. But the prospective terms of rediscounting are vital, when it comes to the *difference* between short and long rates.

moves to the right (as the dotted curve in Fig. 10), but the horizontal parts of the curve are almost the same. Therefore, again, it is this doldrum to the left of the diagram which upsets the classical theory. If *IS* lies to the right, then we can indeed increase employment by increasing the quantity of money; but if *IS* lies to the left, we cannot do so; merely monetary means will not force down the rate of interest any further.

So the General Theory of Employment is the Economics of Depression.

IV

In order to elucidate the relation between Mr. Keynes and the 'Classics', we have invented a little apparatus. It does not appear that we have exhausted the uses of that apparatus, so let us conclude by giving it a little run on its own.

With that apparatus at our disposal, we are no longer obliged to make certain simplifications which Mr. Keynes makes in his exposition. We can reinsert the missing i in the third equation, and allow for any possible effect of the rate of interest upon saving; and, what is much more important, we can call in question the sole dependence of investment upon the rate of interest, which looks rather suspicious in the second equation. Mathematical elegance would suggest that we ought to have I and i in all three equations, if the theory is to be really General. Why not have them there like this:

$$M = L(I, i), \quad I_x = C(I, i), \quad I_x = S(I, i)?$$

Once we raise the question of Income in the second equation, it is clear that it has a very good claim to be inserted. Mr. Keynes is, in fact, only enabled to leave it out at all plausibly by his device of measuring everything in 'wage-units', which means that he allows for changes in the marginal-efficiency-of-capital schedule when there is a change in the level of money wages, but that other changes in Income are deemed not to affect the curve, or at least not in

the same immediate manner. But why draw this distinction?
Surely there is every reason to suppose that an increase in
the demand for consumers' goods, arising from an increase
in employment, will often directly stimulate an increase in
investment, at least as soon as an expectation develops that
the increased demand will continue. If this is so, we ought
to include I in the second equation, though it must be con-
fessed that the effect of I on the marginal efficiency of capital
will be fitful and irregular.

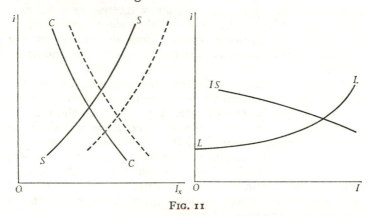

Fig. 11

The Generalized General Theory can then be set out in
this way. Assume first of all a given total money Income. Draw
a curve CC showing the marginal efficiency of capital (in
money terms) at that given Income; a curve SS showing the
supply curve of saving at that *given* Income (Fig. 11). Their
intersection will determine the rate of interest which makes
savings equal to investment at that level of income. This we
may call the 'investment rate'.

If Income rises, the curve SS will move to the right;
probably CC will move to the right too. If SS moves more
than CC, the investment rate of interest will fall; if CC more
than SS, it will rise. (How much it rises and falls, however,
depends upon the elasticities of the CC and SS curves.)

The *IS* curve (drawn on a separate diagram) now shows the relation between Income and the corresponding investment rate of interest. It has to be confronted (as in our earlier constructions) with an *LL* curve showing the relation between Income and the 'money' rate of interest; only we can now generalize our *LL* curve a little. Instead of assuming, as before, that the supply of money is given, we can assume that there is a given monetary system—that up to a point, but only up to a point, monetary authorities will prefer to create new money rather than allow interest rates to rise. Such a generalized *LL* curve will then slope upwards only gradually—the elasticity of the curve depending on the elasticity of the monetary system (in the ordinary monetary sense).

As before, Income and interest are determined where the *IS* and *LL* curves intersect—where the investment rate of interest equals the money rate. Any change in the inducement to invest or the propensity to consume will shift the *IS* curve; any change in liquidity of preference or monetary policy will shift the *LL* curve. If, as the result of such a change, the investment rate is raised above the money rate, Income will tend to rise; in the opposite case, Income will tend to fall; the extent to which Income rises or falls depends on the elasticities of the curves.[1]

When generalized in this way, Mr. Keynes's theory begins to look very like Wicksell's; this is of course hardly surprising.[2] There is indeed one special case where it fits Wicksell's construction absolutely. If there is 'full employment' in the

---

[1] Since $C(I, i) = S(I, i)$,

$$\frac{dI}{di} = -\frac{\partial S/\partial i - \partial C/\partial i}{\partial S/\partial I - \partial C/\partial I}.$$

The savings investment market will not be stable unless $\partial S/\partial i + (-\partial C/\partial i)$ is positive. I think we may assume that this condition is fulfilled.

If $\partial S/\partial i$ is positive, $\partial C/\partial i$ negative, $\partial S/\partial I$ and $\partial C/\partial I$ positive (the most probable state of affairs), we can say that the *IS* curve will be more elastic, the greater the elasticities of the *CC* and *SS* curves, and the larger is $\partial C/\partial I$ relatively to $\partial S/\partial I$. When $\partial C/\partial I > \partial S/\partial I$, the *IS* curve is upward sloping.

[2] Cf. Keynes, *General Theory*, p. 242.

sense that any rise in Income immediately calls forth a rise in money wage rates; then it is *possible* that the CC and SS curves may be moved to the right to exactly the same extent, so that IS is horizontal. (I say possible, because it is not un-likely, in fact, that the rise in the wage level may create a presumption that wages will rise again later on; if so, CC will probably be shifted more than SS, so that IS will be upward sloping.) However that may be, if IS is horizontal, we do have a perfectly Wicksellian construction; the investment rate becomes Wicksell's *natural rate*, for in this case it may be thought of as determined by real causes; if there is a per-fectly elastic monetary system, and the money rate is fixed below the natural rate, there is cumulative inflation; cumula-tive deflation if it is fixed above.

This, however, is now seen to be only one special case; we can use our construction to harbour much wider possi-bilities. If there is a great deal of unemployment, it is very likely that $\partial C/\partial I$ will be quite small; in that case IS can be relied upon to slope downwards. This is the sort of Slump Economics with which Mr. Keynes is largely concerned. But one cannot escape the impression that there may be other conditions when expectations are tinder, when a slight inflationary tendency lights them up very easily. Then $\partial C/\partial I$ may be large and an increase in Income tend to *raise* the investment rate of interest. In these circumstances, the situation is unstable at *any* given money rate; it is only an imperfectly elastic monetary system—a rising LL curve—that can prevent the situation getting out of hand altogether.

These, then, are a few of the things we can get out of our skeleton apparatus. But even if it may claim to be a slight extension of Mr. Keynes's similar skeleton, it remains a terribly rough and ready sort of affair. In particular, the concept of 'Income' is worked monstrously hard; most of our curves are not really determinate unless something is said about the distribution of Income as well as its magnitude. Indeed, what they express is something like a relation between the price-system and the system of interest rates; and you can-not get that into a curve. Further, all sorts of questions about depreciation have been neglected; and all sorts of questions about the timing of the processes under consideration.

8

THE 'CLASSICS' AGAIN[1]

IT is a strange thing that twenty years after the publication of the *General Theory*, doubt should still persist, even among careful thinkers, about the exact nature of the innovations which led Keynes to different *results* from those which had generally been accepted by his predecessors. Some of the innovations of the *General Theory* are innovations of method, which opened the way to new results, or provide better ways of reaching old results; with these I am not here concerned. But there are important cases in which Keynes's predecessors said one thing, and Keynes said exactly the opposite; where Keynes maintains that something is true which earlier economists, who had spoken with authority in their own time, had stated quite definitely to be false. What is the basic reason (or reasons) for this turnabout?

I

The crucial point, as I now feel quite clear, on which the individuality of the Keynes theory depends, is the implication that there are conditions in which the price-mechanism will not 'work'—more specifically, that there are conditions in which the interest-mechanism will not work. The special form in which this appears in the *General Theory* is the doctrine of the *floor* to the rate of interest—the 'liquidity trap' as Sir Dennis Robertson has called it. But there are other possible ways in which interest may not work, which we shall be

[1] A paper which originally appeared (in the *Economic Journal*, 1957) as a review of D. Patinkin, *Money, Interest and Prices* (1st edition); but it was pulled out of shape by the reference to Patinkin, which has now been withdrawn.

considering later. It is very probable that Keynes did not
see this clearly at the time when he was writing;[1] he was still
in two minds whether he believed in curing unemployment
by monetary expansion, or whether he had come to hold that
mere monetary stimulus was liable to be ineffective if it was
not backed up by more direct methods. On the practical
level he was still trying to keep a foot in both camps. But on
the theoretical level he was already committed by the logic
of his system to the second of these alternatives.

In a world where the interest-mechanism can always
operate—where the rate of interest is flexible, and sufficiently
flexible, in either direction, for its movements to have a
significant effect on (saving or) investment—the Keynes
theory is true and the 'classical' theory is true; they lead to
the same results. Though the paths of analysis are different,
the end-results, achieved when all the same things have been
taken into account, are the same. And either analysis can be
put into a general-equilibrium form in which it is directly
apparent that they come to the same thing.

Thus, for instance, Keynes would argue that an increase in
the propensity to save (money wages being fixed) would
diminish employment directly; but he would then qualify this
statement by an admission that the diminished demand for
transactions balances would lower the rate of interest (if
interest is flexible), and that this would have a secondary
effect increasing investment and hence employment—but
to something less than its former level. A properly equipped
'classic' would get to the same result by a different route. He
would argue that the increase in saving would *directly* reduce
the rate of interest, so that employment would increase in
the investment-goods trades as it diminished in the consumption-goods trades; but he could (or should) go on to admit
that the increase in saving would carry with it a diminution
in the velocity of circulation (some of the saving would be
hoarded), so that, with an inelastic monetary system, and the
fixed money wages that are being assumed, there would still

[1] *General Theory*, pp. 201–4.

be a net decline in employment. A general-equilibrium theorist would show the saving operating on interest and employment simultaneously. One can put the systems through their paces in many such ways, and—so long as the interest mechanism functions—one must come in the end to the same result by each method.

Instead of checking over, in the above manner, all the manifold cases which require consideration, it will be more revealing to proceed diagrammatically. I may be allowed to use the apparatus to which I am accustomed myself. So long as money wage-rates are given, it is possible, as I showed many years ago,[1] to express the essence of the Keynes theory on a single diagram. One measures Income (Keynes's Y) along one axis, and interest (r) along the other; one then draws an SI curve[2] (based on the Marginal Efficiency of Capital schedule and the Consumption Function) connecting those levels of Income at which Saving equals Investment, at various rates of interest. Granted that Investment rises as r falls, and Y rises as Investment rises, this must be a downward-sloping curve. We then confront this curve with a LL curve showing the rate of interest at which the demand for money will equal a given supply of money, at each given Income (Y). Granted that the demand for money increases with Y, and diminishes with r (as Keynes maintains), this LL curve will be upward sloping. Equilibrium (which can easily be shown to be a stable equilibrium) is established at the point where these two curves intersect.

As this diagram was originally drawn, it laid excessive weight on the assumption of fixed money wages; even for the elucidation of Keynes, it paid insufficient attention to the possibility of Full Employment. For present purposes, it is essential that that gap should be filled. Suppose that (still assuming our given level of money wages) Full Employment is reached at an income ON. (Refinements about hetero-

[1] Mr. Keynes and the 'Classics', (above, pp. 126–42). See also my *Contribution to the Theory of the Trade Cycle*, ch. xi.
[2] Or IS curve, as I called it in 1937.

geneity of labour supply, and such like, need not concern us here.) Further expansion beyond *ON* must be purely monetary in character, so that in money terms the *SI* curve must be horizontal beyond the point *FE*. But it is more satisfactory (Keynes would no doubt agree) to work from this stage onwards in real terms, so that *Y* is reckoned *in wage-units*. On this convention (adopted in Fig. 12) the *SI* curve will be unaffected until the Full Employment level is reached, but it

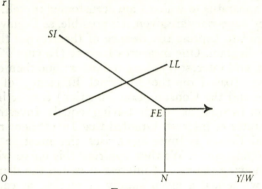

FIG. 12

will then be cut short at the point *FE*. Any attempt to move beyond *FE* will induce a merely inflationary expansion that is *not* represented on the diagram, but of which the arrow that is shown serves as a reminder.

The decision to work in wage-units has no more than this limited effect on the *SI* curve; but its effect on the *LL* curve is more serious. When the price- and wage-level changes the *LL* curve will stay put only if the quantity of money remains unaltered *in terms of wage-units*; but there is in general no reason why it should do so. If the supply of money is fixed in money terms, then (when wages rise) the supply in terms of wage-units contracts, so that the *LL* curve moves to the left. Thus, so long as the supply of money is restrained from expanding (in money terms), wage-inflation must bring its own cure. If, initially, the *LL* curve lies to the right of the *FE* point, the inflation itself will bring it back. (There does, of course, remain the danger that the inflation will have acquired such momentum that the *FE* point is overshot before the leftward movement ceases—but that is not a matter which concerns us here.) Equilibrium will always be reached, if the supply of money is kept under control, at *FE* or on the downward-sloping part of the *SI* curve.

What I want now to emphasize is that the construction so far reached, though it has been expressed in a manner which has a Keynesian tendency, still contains nothing whatever that is inconsistent with 'classical' theory. The only way in which it differs from what was taught by 'classical' economists, from Hume to Marshall and Pigou, is in the assumption that it makes about the behaviour of wages—that they can flex upwards but not downwards; but this is a special assumption that can be incorporated into any theory. Certainly the economists of the past cannot be criticized for not making it, for in their time it would, quite clearly, not have been true. This is not a matter on which there can be any theoretical *contradiction*; it is the kind of change in the exposition of theory which we ought to be making, all the time, in response to changing facts.

If it was desired to apply the above construction to a world in which wages could flex in *both* directions, no major change would have to be made. It would only be necessary to introduce a 'Full Unemployment' point *FU*, beyond which wages would fall, just as they rise beyond the Full Employment point *FE*. Beyond *FU* the curve would be cut off, just as it is cut off at *FE*. If, initially, the *LL* curve lay to the left of *FU*, there would be a fall in prices and wages; but this would *increase* the quantity of money in terms of wage-units, so that the *LL* curve would move to the *right*. Provided that the shape of the *LL* curve is as I have drawn it (Fig. 13), equilibrium must be restored on the sloping part of the *SI* curve—at *FU* or at *FE* or somewhere between them.

The theory which is illustrated in Fig. 13 is, I believe, one form of 'classical' theory; one can recognize it in Hume[1] and Thornton,[2] to say the least. But it is not the whole of the classical theory on this matter, for there is an important respect in which it is unsatisfactory. It pays insufficient attention to the element of time.

It assumes (justly, for the circumstances with which it had to deal) that wages can flex in both directions; but it does at the same time permit a certain rigidity. Over a certain range,

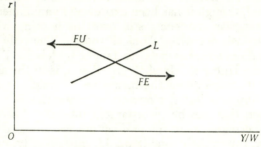

Fig. 13

wages are rigid. But though it is true that in a free market for labour, wages do possess a certain rigidity, that rigidity is not merely a matter of the intensity of the demand; it is also a matter of the time for which it lasts. If *FE* is taken to be the point at which wages will rise *at once*, when that intensity of demand is reached (and similarly for *FU*), it would be nonsense not to suppose that the two points would be quite far apart; but if they are understood as the points at which wages will move if demand is maintained at such a position for some considerable time, then (it would be reasonable to suppose) they might be quite close together. Thus while the classical theory has a short-period form, in which it is representable by Fig. 13, it also has a long-period form (which, admittedly, tended in practice to engross far too much attention) in which all prices, including wages, are taken to

[1] 'Of Money' in *Essays*, Oxford University Press, pp. 289-302.
[2] *Paper Credit* (ed. Hayek), pp. 118-19, 236. (See below, pp. 172-88).

be *completely* flexible, so that *FE* and *FU* coincide with one another. The *SI* curve with which we began has then collapsed to a single point.

Once this collapse has occurred, we get no further advantage from working in wage-units, and it is easier to revert to the measurement in terms of money with which we began. The classical *long-period* theory (or *full-equilibrium* theory, it might be better to call it) is then representable by Fig. 14,

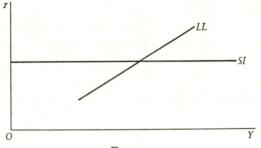

Fig. 14

in which *Y* is again expressed in money terms, while the *SI* curve has become a horizontal line, movement along which represents nothing else but a merely monetary expansion (or contraction). The *LL* curve is now fixed in position, as soon as the money supply (in money-units) is given. Here at last we have the rate of interest solely determined in real terms (by productivity and thrift); for the height of the horizontal line is solely dependent upon the real factors in the system; it cannot be affected by the position of the *LL* curve. All that the *LL* curve here determines is the level of money incomes. The famous 'dichotomy' between real and monetary economics has appeared.

It must be freely admitted that 'classical' economists, from Turgot and Smith onwards (long before Ricardo), did work far too much in terms of this full-equilibrium model; the qualifications due to the relative rigidity of wages (and some other prices), which should have been evident even from their experience,[1] did not receive enough attention. But, after all, they did receive some attention, and not only from Hume and Thornton. Even within the framework of classical analysis, it was possible to get a little farther on.

If one compares the two 'classical' diagrams which we have drawn (Figs. 13 and 14), the interesting phenomenon which comes out is the tendency for an increase in the supply of money to produce a temporary equilibrium in which employment is higher, and *the rate of interest lower*, than in the corresponding full equilibrium. But this tendency could be analysed on classical lines, and was in fact analysed by some classical economists, from Bentham onwards, in their theory of 'forced saving'.[2] An increased supply of money would temporarily increase saving (even in real terms) through its distributional effects; this would force down the rate of interest, and (as was obvious to a believer in the Wage Fund) it would temporarily increase employment. Here again there is no fundamental opposition between the classical model and the Keynes model. What is, of course, true is that many classical economists disliked these consequences of their theory (it is amusing to watch Mill squirming to avoid them),[3] so that the full-equilibrium theory always received more attention than the short-period theory. After 1850, with the decline in the Wage Fund (a decline which was itself a symptom of lack of interest in short-period phenomena), the concentration of interest on our Fig. 14, rather than our Fig. 13, is very complete.

II

All the same, it is at this point in the story that more must be said about the *LL* curve. I have drawn the *LL* curve with a

---

[1] "In many places the money price of labour remains uniformly the same for half a century together." (Smith, *Wealth of Nations*, Cannan ed., vol. i, p. 76).

[2] Cf. Hayek, 'Note on the Development of the Doctrine of Forced Saving', *Quarterly Journal of Economics*, 1932; also Schumpeter, *History of Economic Analysis*, pp. 723–5.

[3] J. S. Mill, *Principles*, book iii, ch. 23; see Schumpeter's comments in the passage just quoted. Also, below, p. 163.

gentle rightward slope; this, I think, is the correct form which it would take for an economist who recognized Keynes's *transactions motive*, and also his *precautionary motive*, but not his *speculative motive* (to which we shall come later). And that, I think, is how it would appear to the 'properly equipped classical economist' whom I am using in this paper as an instrument of analysis. In fact, one can find the precautionary motive already in Thornton;[1] there are traces of it in Marshall;[2] after long travail, it emerges in Walras.[3] Any of these writers should have recognized that the demand for money has some elasticity against the rate of interest; and that, in our terminology, should have given his *LL* curve a rightward tilt.

A less perspicacious economist, who recognized the transactions motive only (or some equivalent to it) would draw his *LL* curve simply vertical; if, as is only too probable, he also looked only at full equilibrium, so that his *SI* curve was horizontal (as in our Fig. 14), his whole 'diagram' would have reduced to two perpendicular straight lines. The 'dichotomy' is then complete; real and monetary theories have completely fallen apart. This is the case of the crude quantity theorist. But to suggest that such crude quantity theorizing was characteristic of the more subtle minds among the older economists is a caricature of the history of economic thought.

Yet it is interesting to notice that one could be a crude quantity theorist, so far as the *LL* curve is concerned, and at the same time one could admit a distinction between temporary and full equilibrium (Figs. 13 and 14), with its consequence that an increase in the money supply can, in the short period, have a stimulating effect. So far as the real effects of monetary causes are concerned, the slope of the *LL* curve does not greatly signify.[4] Where it does signify is in the other

---

[1] *Paper Credit*, pp. 96–97.
[2] *Official Papers*, p. 268; see Patinkin, op. cit., p. 418.
[3] Patinkin, pp. 377–412.
[4] This has often been misunderstood, as in the passage from Schumpeter previously noted. It is the assumption of instantaneous flexibility in wage-rates, the lack of distinction between temporary and full

direction, when the initiating cause of the change comes from the *real* side.

If one's *LL* curve is crudely vertical, a rise in the *SI* curve (due to an increase in the propensity to invest or a fall in the propensity to save) will *simply* raise the rate of interest; and this is true, whether one looks only at full equilibrium (Fig. 14) or whether one admits the possibility of a temporary divergence from that equilibrium (Fig. 13). But if one admits a precautionary motive (giving one's *LL* curve a rightward slant), then one should conclude that these real shifts will have monetary effects; the money value of income will be affected in the full equilibrium, while in the temporary equilibrium there may be effects on employment. I have not been able to find that there was any early economist who can be claimed as having thought the thing through right to this point; it looks as if it had to wait for Pigou and Robertson. Nevertheless, it is clear that one *can* go so far as this without straying outside the bounds of 'classical' theory. One can still argue, in the old way, that the savings-investment change raises the rate of interest; and then qualify by observing that the rise in interest releases money balances, thus increasing effective demand.[1] Though we have got so near to Keynes, it is not yet *necessary* to argue the matter in a Keynesian manner.

There is, however, a further point. Though a full recognition of the role of the precautionary motive may have had to wait for the modern Cambridge school, the monetary effect of real causes could be recognized, and was recognized, within the classical theory, in another way. It was understood by Thornton (and even by Ricardo[2]) that a rise in the *SI* curve would ordinarily lead to an expansion of credit; whether one reckons that expansion as an increase in the

equilibrium in the labour market, not adherence to a quantity theory, which prevents one from having a monetary theory of employment.

[1] This, of course, is Pigou's proposed way of arguing. See, for instance, his *Lapses from Full Employment*.

[2] 'The applications to the bank for money depend on the comparison between the rate of profits that may be made by the employment of it and the rate at which they are willing to lend it.' (*Principles*, ch. xxvii: ed. Sraffa, vol. i, p. 364.)

supply of money, or as an increase in the velocity of circulation of money, is a question of the definition of money which one is using. If one adopts the former interpretation, recognition of the monetary effects of real causes can be reconciled with a formal adherence to the quantity theory in the strict sense. Nevertheless, it is clear that the other interpretation was always open, and with the rather unformalized banking system of the early nineteenth century it was a natural interpretation. In Wicksell's case, in view of what he says about 'virtual velocity of circulation',[1] I cannot believe it was wholly absent. Whether one draws up one's *LL* curve on the assumption that the quantity of money is constant in one sense, or in another sense, or whether one merely assumes some constancy in the pattern of behaviour of the monetary system, is in a certain sense a matter of detail. The step from Wicksell to Keynes, vital step though it is, remains from some perspectives a very short step indeed.

III

In Wicksell, the *LL* curve is horizontal, because the banking system is operating in such a way as to maintain a constant rate of interest. If we put this constant market rate against an *SI* curve which has already degenerated (as in our Fig. 14) into a constant natural rate, we get Wicksell's famous construction. 'If the market rate is below the natural rate . . .' it all follows. Keynes is using the same kind of construction for the study of temporary equilibrium. But he is maintaining that the *LL* curve becomes horizontal (over certain ranges) not because the banking system is choosing to make it horizontal, but because it is unable to act in any other way. It is not merely that the interest-mechanism may be prevented from operating; there are also circumstances in which it cannot be made to work. We then become *obliged* to analyse what happens in a Keynesian manner.

So long as this possibility is ruled out, we are at liberty to

[1] *Lectures*, vol. ii, pp. 67 ff.

say that saving and investment determine the rate of interest, and that the effects on employment (or on inflation and deflation) depend on the way in which the monetary system reacts to an interest change. Or we are at liberty to regard interest and 'income' as being simultaneously determined, on general-equilibrium lines. But once the Keynes case has to be allowed for, both of these techniques fail us. If the rate of interest is liable to be 'pegged' (not by any action of the monetary authority, but in the nature of the case), then we must treat the effect on income (and employment) as the primary effect, which may or may not be modified by indirect repercussions through the interest rate. It is no longer possible to use the general-equilibrium bridge to show that classical and Keynesian theories come to the same thing.

It should, however, be added in conclusion that the Keynes theory would be less important than it is if this were the only limiting case on which it threw light. The interest-mechanism may fail to operate, not only because the rate of interest may itself be insensitive to real changes, but also because (again over certain ranges and in certain circumstances) saving and investment may themselves be insensitive to changes in the interest rate. A Keynesian (non-classical) situation may arise, not only because the LL curve may be horizontal over certain stretches, but because the (short-period) SI curve may, over certain stretches, be vertical. A vertical SI curve, impinging upon a sloping LL curve, would show the rate of interest rising when investment increased; but the rise in interest would be a matter of mere financial interest, without real effects. It is because of their desire to cover this case, quite as much as the other, that modern Keynesians are convinced that Keynes, unlike the 'classics', did make the right approach. It is true that when the two theories are properly understood, and fully worked out, they largely overlap; but they do not overlap all the way, and when they fail to do so, the Keynes theory has the wider coverage.

9

MONETARY THEORY AND HISTORY—
AN ATTEMPT AT PERSPECTIVE[1]

I HAVE attempted, on two previous occasions, to elucidate the relation between Keynes and those whom he called 'classics'. The method that was employed in those papers[2] was analytical; analysis was one of the things that needed to be done; I believe that the analytical method, up to a point, did justify itself. It has nevertheless left me in some ways dissatisfied. The question is not merely analytical, it is also historical. What did the pre-Keynesian writers say, and why did they say it? In order to complete the discussion, there are some further matters in this direction which need to be explored.

'Classics', as used by Keynes, was a confusing description. Before Keynes (and even since Keynes, by those who are not specially concerned with Keynesian controversy), 'classical economics' has been used in a different and more restricted sense. What we otherwise mean by classical economics is the economics of Adam Smith, Ricardo, and their contemporaries; not the economics of those whom we have now had to call the 'neo-classics'—those who flourished in the three-quarters of a century before 1936. Keynes certainly means his 'classics' to include the neo-classics; it may indeed be some of the latter whom his cap most exactly fits. But I think that he spoke of them all as 'classics' because he perceived (quite rightly perceived) that some of the things he was attacking came down from Smith and Ricardo, especially perhaps Ricardo, whom he was right in identifying as the

[1] Given as the Edward Shann lecture, Perth, Western Australia, in February 1967.
[2] Essays 7 and 8 above.

chief originator of what he called the classical tradition. It was indeed the old classical period that was the formative period. But if one goes back to that period it is not just this 'classical' tradition that is forming; other things were happening as well. There were differences, or qualifications; I believe that we understand much better what happened if we give some weight to them. For they do not only show how there came to be an 'orthodoxy' for Keynes to attack; they also throw light upon the Keynesian orthodoxy which has so largely replaced it. It is very desirable, at the stage we have now reached (and even, as we shall see, in relation to our own contemporary problems) that we should make some effort to get the whole story into proper focus.

I

Monetary theory is less abstract than most economic theory; it cannot avoid a relation to reality, which in other economic theory is sometimes missing. It belongs to monetary history, in a way that economic theory does not always belong to economic history. Indeed it does so in two ways which need to be distinguished.

It is noticeable, on the one hand, that a large part of the best work on Money is topical. It has been prompted by particular episodes, by particular experiences of the writer's own time. All theorizing is simplifying, cutting out the unimportant and leaving what is thought to be important, in the hope that by simplifying we may increase understanding. Sometimes what is sought is a general understanding; but with monetary theory it is more often a particular understanding—an understanding directed towards a particular problem, normally a problem of the time at which the work in question is written. So monetary theories arise out of monetary disturbances. This is obviously true of the *General Theory*, which is the book of the Great Depression—the World Depression—of the nineteen-thirties; it is also true of Keynes's other version, the *Treatise on Money*, which differs from the *General Theory* quite largely because it is directed at a different contemporary problem. Though the *Treatise* was published in 1930, after the Depression had begun, it must largely have been written earlier. Its world is not the world of the Depression, it is the world of the Restored Gold Standard. Its problem is how the Restored Gold Standard is to be made to work. Now much the same is true of Ricardo and his contemporaries, a century earlier.

Ricardo's monetary writings (the earliest is dated 1808, and he died in 1823) cover a period of War Inflation, in the last stages of the British war against Napoleon, and a period of reconstruction, and attempted stabilization, after the Peace. His problems are the problems of those years. Thus his work, like Keynes's, was the result of a challenge—a challenge from contemporary experience. It is possible that one reason why monetary theory did get a bit ossified in its neo-classical phase is that in that phase there seemed to be no similar challenge. At least in the seventies and eighties, when Marshall (the greatest of the neo-classicals) could have responded to a challenge, it was just not there; you could not get much of a kick out of bi-metallism! You cannot get brilliant answers to a dull question-paper; and the question-paper that was set to Marshall by his monetary facts really was a bit dull.

That topicality is one way in which monetary theory is historically conditioned; but there is another also.

Throughout the whole time—back before Ricardo, forward after Keynes—money itself has been evolving. The change from metallic money to paper money is obvious; but there are other things which have gone with that change, of even greater importance, which are not so easy to recognize and to assess. Even if we say that metallic money has given place to credit money, we are still not getting to the bottom of what has happened. For credit money is just a part of a whole credit structure that extends outside money; it is closely interwoven with a whole system of debts and credits, of claims and obligations, some of which are money, some of which are not, and some of which are on the edge of being money. The obvious change in the money medium, from 'full-bodied' coins to notes and bank deposits, is just a part of a wider development, the development of a financial system. This has taken the form of the growth of financial institutions, not just banks, but other 'financial intermediaries' as well; it has carried with it a fundamental change in the financial activities of governments. In the course of these changes there has been a change in the whole character of the monetary system. In a world of banks and insurance companies, money markets and stock exchanges, money is quite a different thing from what it was before these institutions came into being.

This evolution has been going on ever since the time of Ricardo (its beginnings, of course, are much earlier); it clearly called, as it proceeded, for a radical revision of monetary theory. As the actual system changed, the theoretical simplification ought to have changed with it. We can now see that it did not change sufficiently; there was a lag. But the reason for the lag was not just laziness or sleepiness; there was an obstacle to be overcome.

On the theoretical level—in terms of basic principles—the evolution that was occurring had two aspects. From one of them it was a natural piece of economizing. Metallic money is an expensive way of performing a simple function; why waste resources in digging up gold from the ground when pieces of paper (or mere book entries) which can be provided, and transported, at a fraction of the cost will do as well? That is the reason why the credit system grows: that it provides a medium of exchange at much lower cost. But on the other side there is the penalty that the credit system is an unstable system. It rests upon confidence and trust; when trust is absent it can just shrivel up. It is unstable in the other direction too; when there is too much 'confidence' or optimism it can explode in bursts of speculation. Thus in order for a credit system to work smoothly, it needs an institutional framework which shall restrain it on the one hand, and shall support it on the other. To find a framework which can be relied on to give support when it is needed, and to impose restraint just when it is needed, is very difficult; I do not think it has ever been perfectly solved. Even in this day we do not really know the answer.

II

When Ricardo and his contemporaries saw this problem (some of them, as we shall see, did certainly begin to see it) it frightened them quite a bit. So they tried to hack their way out.

At their date, it must be remembered, the evolution of the credit system had not gone very far. Thus it was natural still to regard the metallic money as primary; the notes and bills (which already existed) as a tiresome, but secondary, qualification. If only the secondary money would behave like primary money, there would be no trouble! So let us try to make it behave like primary money. Then we can carry on in our thinking with a simple, easily understandable, primary money model.

That, in effect, is what Ricardo did. But it is not enough to recognize that his model is a metallic money model. We should still ask: as a metallic money model, for a system without developed credit, was it right? Would it be true, even in a world where all borrowing and lending was long-term borrowing and lending (for that, at the least, must be assumed if we are to have no credit)[1] that interest rates will be entirely determined by saving and investment, that the level of activity will be solely determined by the real factors in the system, and that the quantity of money will solely act upon the level of prices? These are the 'classical' doctrines, which we associate with Ricardo. It is evident that Ricardo relied upon them as an approximation to reality; but I wonder whether

[1] A more exact statement of the necessary conditions will be found above, p. 43.

even he, even for his metallic money model, thought that they were *exactly* true.

For there are writings, serious and intelligent writings, which were available to Ricardo (which indeed we can be quite sure that he must have read), and in which some at least of the qualifications are quite clearly set out. The most striking of these is the essay 'Of Money' by David Hume. Hume, of course, is most famous as a philosopher; but he was no mean economist also. He was a close friend of Adam Smith, but his work on economics is earlier than Smith's; it was Smith who learned from Hume, not the other way about. For Hume, writing in 1750, it was natural to assume a purely metallic money; for the growth of the credit system, though it had begun, was in his day at a much earlier stage than it was in Ricardo's. But his analysis of the working of a monetary system is not simply what Keynes would have called 'classical'. For Hume the Quantity Theory of Money is *an equilibrium condition.*

Money [he says] is nothing but the representation of labour and commodities, and serves only as a method of rating or estimating them. Where coin is in greater plenty—as a greater quantity of it is required to represent the same quantity of goods—it can have no effect, either good or bad, taking a nation within itself; any more than it would make an alteration in a merchant's books, if instead of the Arabian method of notation, which requires few characters, he should make use of the Roman, which requires a great many.[1]

That, for Hume, is the main point; the *classical*, Quantity Theory, point. But Hume goes on:

Notwithstanding this conclusion, which must be allowed just, it is certain that since the discovery of the mines in America, industry has increased in all the nations of Europe, except in the possessors of those mines; and this may justly be ascribed, among other reasons, to the increase of gold and silver. Accordingly we

---

[1] Hume, *Essays*, Oxford University Press, pp. 292–3.

find that in every kingdom, into which money begins to flow in greater abundance than formerly, everything takes on a new face; labour and industry gain life; the merchant becomes more enterprising, and even the farmer follows his plough with greater alacrity and attention. . . .

To account then for this phenomenon, we must consider, that though the high price of commodities be a necessary consequence of the increase of gold and silver, yet it follows not immediately upon that increase; but some time is required before the money circulates through the whole state, and makes its effect be felt on all ranks of people. At first, no alteration is perceived; by degrees the price rises, first of one commodity, then of another; till the whole at last reaches a just proportion with the new quantity of specie which is in the kingdom. In my opinion, it is only in this interval or intermediate situation, between the acquisition of money and the rise of prices, that the increasing quantity of gold and silver is favourable to industry.[1]

Putting the point in our language, the Quantity theory is valid as a long-term equilibrium condition; but in the short period, while the supply of money is increasing, the increase can be a real stimulus. Now the interesting question is: if Ricardo had been challenged, and had been held to it, would he—could he—have said anything different?

There is one piece of evidence which suggests that after all he would not. It is evidently implied by what Hume says about the stimulus of monetary expansion that the effect of monetary contraction will be the reverse. If the supply of money is reduced, or if money is taken out of circulation by hoarding, prices will fall; but while they are falling, business will be depressed. Now though Ricardo (so far as I know) never admitted this as a principle, he acted as if he believed it. For though he was prepared to accept some fall in prices, after the war (through which he had been living for so long) was over, in order to achieve what he thought was the great good of monetary stability, he was very much concerned to ensure that the fall in prices should not be unnecessarily

[1] Ibid., pp. 293–4.

large. That was the purpose of his famous 'Ingot Plan' which was designed to prevent an excessive fall in the money in circulation.[1] I do not see why he should have been so bothered upon this, if he regarded money prices—the course of money prices over time—as having no *real* importance.

Quite a number of things will fit into place if we suppose that the classical economists, of this important and in so many ways constructive period, did have some such short-period theory, somewhere at the back of their minds, though they preferred not to emphasize it. One can see several reasons why they should have preferred not to emphasize it.

There was a special reason in Ricardo's own case, that he was the great creator of the static equilibrium method in economics; he was showing, for the first time, how much could be done with that method; it was his method, and he was reluctant to turn away from it. Not only here, but in many other applications, he tended to rush from one equilibrium to another much too quick. Then there is the point, which I have already mentioned, that the monetary theory of that time was oriented towards a particular practical problem, the restoration of a particular kind of stability, a problem that seemed eminently suitable for analysis in equilibrium terms. But there was also another reason, the most important of all. They were terribly afraid that if too much weight were given to short-period effects, it would play into the hands of crude inflationists. The long-period, it would be said, is just a succession of short-periods. Why not keep the stimulus going, when the first dose is exhausted, by another dose? They were afraid of that question, for they did not know the answer to it. Yet they felt in their bones that the suggestion in it was wrong.

Nowadays, I think, we know the answer. We know it in theory, and we have seen it confirmed in practice. Inflation does give a stimulus, but the stimulus is greatest when the

[1] The point is well discussed in R. S. Sayers, 'Ricardo's Views on Monetary Questions' (*Papers in English Monetary History*, ed. Ashton and Sayers).

inflation starts—when it starts from a condition that has been non-inflationary. If the inflation continues, people get adjusted to it. But when people are adjusted to it, when they *expect* rising prices, the mere occurrence of what has been expected is no longer stimulating. Nor can the fade-out be prevented by accelerating the inflation; for acceleration of inflation can be expected too. It is perfectly possible to have an 'inflationary equilibrium', in which prices go on rising, even for years, more or less as they are expected to rise; but then there is no stimulus. In real terms, in terms of production and even of employment, the economy may be very depressed. We have seen examples of this in our time, in South America and in East Asia, in Argentina and in Indonesia, for instance; they are not pretty. The Classical Economists were quite right in refusing to look that way, though they did not quite know just why they were refusing.

You may ask for some evidence that this really was their state of minds. I can say that I know one very eminent nineteenth-century economist in whom the statement of it is almost explicit—so nearly explicit as to be readily recognizable; this is John Stuart Mill. There is no doubt at all that Mill did have a short-period theory such as I have been describing. He has written it out for us himself, in his essay on the 'Influence of Consumption upon Production' (in his *Essays on Unsettled Questions*). There is no doubt at all that when Mill wrote that essay he was on what we have been calling Hume's side. But it is a remarkable thing that when we turn to Mill's *Principles* (1848—the *Essays* were published in 1844, but are stated to have been written earlier), we find no reference at all to the argument of the essay. In the *Principles* (see especially the chapter on 'Excess of Supply') Mill appears, on all this side, to be just a hard-boiled 'classic'. The argument of the essay is not withdrawn, but it is just not there. I feel sure that we can best explain Mill's position by supposing that he always held to what he had said in the essay, but he did not want to emphasize it, for he held that it was *dangerous*.

III

All this can be said before we come (at all seriously) to the evolution of credit. But in fact, even in Ricardo's time—and still more by the time of Mill, a generation later—the development of credit had gone quite far. In trying to treat the monetary system as if it was a metallic system, or could be forced into the mould of a metallic system, Ricardo was looking backward. The monetary system in terms of which he was thinking was already, in his day, a thing of the past.

There was at least one of his contemporaries to whom this was quite familiar. Ricardo must certainly have read the 'Enquiry into the Nature and Effects of the Paper Credit of Great Britain', by Henry Thornton (1802—six years earlier than any of Ricardo's writings); but he passed it by. Thornton has a short-period theory, not unlike Hume's; but it is worked out in terms of a credit economy. Thornton's is in fact the best analysis of the working of a credit system which was given by any of the older economists. As a short-period theory, it can be rewritten in a form which brings it quite close to Keynes.[1]

For Thornton does not only recognize (as Hume had done) that in the short period monetary causes may have real effects; he also recognized that in a credit system the reverse can happen. Real causes have monetary effects. A credit system will expand automatically if there are real causes making for an expansion in activity (more or less what Keynes was later to call a rise in the marginal efficiency of capital); it will contract automatically if there is a panic (involving a sharp rise in Liquidity Preference), or if there are changes in the demand for capital which make for contraction. Some of these expansions and contractions are desirable, some highly undesirable. Thornton accordingly held that a credit system must be *managed*. It must be managed by a Central Bank, whose operations must be determined by judgement, and cannot be reduced to procedure by a mechanical rule.

[1] Below, pp. 174–188.

The objectives to which Thornton thought this management should be directed were quite complex; it is most interesting to find that the avoidance of unnecessary unemployment does find a place among them.[1] But the weighting which he gives to different objectives is not unnaturally very different from the weighting which would have been given by Keynes.[2] I need not go into that; the thing on which I want to insist is that Thornton does believe in the necessity of monetary management; on that crucial matter he is on the same side as Keynes—on the opposite side from Ricardo.

Now where did Mill stand on that point? In the light of what I have already said about Mill, that is quite an interesting question. Mill was writing after Ricardo, and after Thornton; there is no doubt that he was acquainted with the work of both. (There is quite a long passage from Thornton's book that is quoted in full in Mill's *Principles*.[3]) Mill was perfectly well aware that he was dealing with what had become a credit economy. Though he did not have Thornton's practical experience, he had good observers of the financial scene[4] on whose work he could draw; and that a mighty change had occurred was by his time unmistakable. Ricardo had died in 1823; there followed in 1825 the first of that notable series of credit crises which mark the economic history of nineteenth-century England (1825, 1839, 1847, 1857, 1866)—demonstrations of the instability of credit which could not be overlooked. This period of credit crises (much more distinctive as credit crises than some of those which have marked later 'trade cycles') was the period during which Mill was writing. He had to take a line about them.

The analysis which Mill gives of the working of credit expansion is really rather good. He saw that it was likely to get started, not by an expansion of bank credit, but by an expansion of trade credit, without the banks (or the main

[1] Below, p. 178.   [2] Below, pp. 180 ff.
[3] pp. 515–19 (Ashley edition), pp. 531–4 (Toronto edition).
[4] Especially Tooke and Fullarton.

banks) being at that stage much involved. As the boom develops, it requires to be fortified by more secure forms of credit, so the pressure is carried back from the circumference to the centre of the banking system. It is essential, at that point, that the centre should hold firm; it must protect itself, but only in order to be able to spread security around it. Because he understands that this is the way the system works, Mill is unable to follow Ricardo in looking for mechanical rules by which credit is to be controlled; it can only be controlled by quite subtle appreciation of the 'feel' of the market, by monetary *policy*. In all this Mill is on the same side as Thornton; he believes in monetary management.

Yet Mill's idea of monetary management seems oddly one-sided. He is concerned to prevent booms; but he seems much less concerned to prevent slumps. One must clearly not attribute this to any lack of sensitivity to the suffering caused by slumps; for Mill is outstanding among the older economists for his social sympathy. It does, however, seem to be explicable in terms of his particular experience. The slumps of his time followed on directly from the crises; they seemed obviously traceable to the disorganization caused by the crisis. Once that disorganization was set right, trade recovered. It was natural to conclude that if the booms could be prevented, if credit could be prevented from over-expanding, the slumps would be prevented too. That is a point (of course) on which a Keynesian economist would refuse to follow him. Mill, I think, just took it for granted; for in his time things did look just like that. It did not seem to be necessary to inquire further.

IV

I can now conclude what I have to say about these old Classical Economists. It is an old story; but I have tried to show that it is a significant story. There is much more to it than the formation of an orthodoxy. The Classical Economists did not all say the same thing. There were differences between them, and some of the differences which then came up for the first time are still important.

There were, at the least, two strands in classical economics. There was one (represented, roughly speaking, by Ricardo and his followers) which maintained that all would be well if by some device credit money could be made to behave like metallic money; there was another (represented, so far as I have taken the story, by Thornton and Mill) which held that credit money must be managed, even though (as was admitted) it is difficult to manage it. This is a major difference, and it has outlasted Keynes. In this sense we still have Ricardians among us. When Milton Friedman tells us that we should have 'a legislated rule instructing the monetary authority to achieve a specified rate of growth in the stock of money',[1] he is being Ricardian. When Jacques Rueff[2] tries to push us into revaluing gold, in order to replace credit money (if only in international transactions) by gold transfers, he is being Ricardian. But this Ricardian strand is only one strand in 'classical' monetary theory; we have Thornton and Mill to prove the contrary.

What happened to these two strands, after the time of Mill, in the neo-classical phase? I must here be very brief. What mainly happened, I think, was this. It was the Ricardian which remained the official doctrine; or perhaps one should say that many things which only make sense in Ricardian terms remained official doctrine. It survived quite sufficiently to be presentable as *the* classical theory for Keynes to attack. Bankers talked Ricardo in their speeches. Descriptions of the monetary system were given in textbooks—in terms of cash ratios, fiduciary issues, and so on—by which the quite fully developed credit system which then existed was translated into Ricardian terms. That, however, was theory; in practice it was the Thornton–Mill school which won out. On strict Ricardian principles, there should have been no need for Central Banks. A Currency Board, working on a rule, should

---

[1] *Capitalism and Freedom*, p. 54.
[2] In many current speeches.

have been enough; but in fact, during this period, there was a growth of Central Banks. There was quite odd double-talk about it. The Bank of England itself was supposed to be Ricardianized by the Bank Charter Act of 1844, which divided it into an Issue Department, that was just to be a Currency Board, and a Banking Department that was to differ little from an ordinary bank. But that was not in fact what happened. The Banking Department became a Central Bank, which, at least to a limited extent, did exercise monetary policy. It had to be cautious about it, since it was not in accordance with official doctrine that it should do so. I think nevertheless that there is no doubt that that is what it did.[1]

This was indeed an odd situation; why did it persist? I think it suited the bankers very well to represent themselves, and even to think of themselves, as passive—just keeping to the 'rules'. For if it had been suspected that they were actively controlling, people would have asked: what right have they to control? Their actions are affecting everyone, affecting everyone (on occasion) very deeply. What right have they, who have not come up through the regular channels of democratic government, to arrogate to themselves such power? So it was useful to them to keep a screen in front of them. Once it was suspected that they were exercising control, their right to control was bound to be called in question. And so, in the end, it proved.

V

That Anti-Banker revolution was one aspect of the 'Keynesian Revolution' as it worked out in practice; but it was mixed up with the other aspect, concerning the kind of control that should be exercised, not who should exercise it. To this I must now turn.

The kind of banking control that Mill envisaged was directed against excessive expansion, not the other way about. I have suggested that in leaning that way, Mill may

[1] Sayers, *Bank of England Operations, 1890–1914.*

have been influenced by his particular experience, by the conditions of the time when he lived; but when we come to Keynes, is there not something of a similar possibility? The *General Theory* was written in the World Depression; even the twenties, when Keynes was writing the *Treatise*, were in England years of semi-slump, or of a boom that misfired. It was natural for Keynes, writing when he did, to take as his base a Depressed economy. His practical problem was emergence from Depression; he looked at the world from a Depression point of view. I am myself quite sufficiently Keynesian to be convinced the Mill kind of control (control which can be exercised by a Central Bank, if it is allowed to exercise it) is by no means enough. But the picture one so easily gets from Keynes, of an economy which will always be under-functioning, unless it is boosted by deliberate expansionary policy, seems to me to be just as one-sided. Ideas which arose in the thirties, and which were appropriate in the thirties, have been carried over, through Keynes's influence, into a world where they do not at all so obviously belong.

However that may be, we have unquestionably learned from Keynes that control through banking is one-sided. It can be effective against inflation and over-expansion; against over-contraction it is relatively powerless. Banks can restrict expansion by refusing to lend; but they cannot force expansion just by offering to lend, on whatever easy terms. It can be that business is feeling so dismal that even on the most favourable possible terms (which are consistent with the banking system making any sort of a profit) loans will not be taken up. (Even so, it is possible for a follower of Mill to retort[1] that this is a very odd state of mind for business men to be in; it must be due to some cause. It must be due to some obstruction in the business circulation, surplus stocks that can and will be worked off, bad debts that can and will be settled; the most that is needed is some help on the way to this natural recovery.) Keynes has nevertheless clearly shown

[1] As I think Dennis Robertson might have done, more or less.

that a depressed economy can be boosted by government spending; and once that is granted, the way to the acceptance of government spending as a *general* booster is hard to resist.

Two general reflections about the post-Keynesian world, which seem to arise out of what I have been saying, may be made in conclusion.

(1) There was a first phase—I think one can now say that it was just a first phase—in which it seemed to be a simple matter for the whole control of economic activity to be taken over by the government budget. This was the heyday of 'Fiscal Policy'. If there was a tendency to contraction, more should be spent; if there was a tendency to over-expansion, taxation should be raised. For a while this did not work badly; but it was an arrangement that had its defects. When the principle is so crudely stated, the defects are rather obvious.

It is easy enough for Government to spend more; that is a simple and popular policy. Some sorts of taxes (taxes that will be paid by people whose votes you don't want) are also popular. But the supply of such convenient taxes tends to give out; control by unpopular taxes is a different matter. When the Keynesian prescription calls upon the Minister to impose unpopular taxes, he begins to long for the old days, when he had a Banker behind whom he could hide. 'This business of monetary control', he will be saying, 'is a technical matter. If I deal with it by fiscal policy, though I can say that I am taking the advice of my experts (my economic advisers and so on), I have to take the responsibility myself for these nasty decisions. It would be much better to let the experts do the job themselves.' So he makes passes to hand it back to the bankers. But he cannot really hand it back to the Bankers, for everyone knows that he controls the Bankers. They are no longer in a position to carry out an independent monetary policy, as they could do—to some limited extent— in former times. What happens is that the control gets lost between them. The control—the Keynesian control—cannot be properly exercised until there is a government that is strong enough to take unpopular measures, and to assume responsibility for them.

In this last passage, I (in my turn) have no doubt been influenced—perhaps over-influenced—by recent experience in Britain. Still I think that the situation is one that can occur elsewhere, and may indeed have occurred elsewhere on some occasions. It is asking quite a lot of a government that it should continue, year in and year out, to maintain a Keynesian control, in both directions.

(2) The other thing on which I want to say something is the international side. This, in its turn, splits up into two parts. In one of them we are looking outwards, from the point of view of the single nation, at its international economic relations. In the other we are looking at the well-being of the international economy as a whole. This latter may appear so remote as hardly to deserve attention; but it is not in fact to the advantage of any single nation that it should be forgotten, and left to look after itself.

In the old days, when monetary control was exercised by Central Bankers, their primary concern was the stability of the currency in terms of foreign exchange. That objective, in the new era, has been deposed from its old position. It was recognized, even in the initial Charter of the IMF, that stability of foreign exchange was not so sacred an object as Central Bankers had tried to make it in former times. Arrangements were made for agreed adjustment of exchange rates on the occasion of what was called a 'Fundamental Disequilibrium'. I would in no way question that this is indeed a real problem, a problem which the world has not (as yet) done much to solve. I would nevertheless maintain that it has been quite over-shadowed by another, by the inflations (active and creeping inflations) which are traceable, not to 'Fundamental Disequilibrium', but to the implementation of pseudo-Keynesian policies by weak and irresolute governments. It is this which has been the main cause of exchange instability, and—what maybe is even worse—of feared exchange instability. There is widespread fear of exchange instability, just because, in the Keynesian epoch, the impression has got around that exchange depreciation, or devaluation, does not matter all that much.

I think it does matter. It may sometimes be necessary, as the least evil among a choice of evils. But it is an evil, which should not be regarded, as it is so often regarded at present, as a normal and natural way out.

The reason why it is an evil becomes apparent when we look at the matter from the other angle, that of the International Economy. The story which I have been telling in terms of those old characters—Thornton and Mill and Ricardo—is repeating itself, in our day, on the international stage. There is the same movement from metallic money (gold) to credit money, going on there too. There is the same problem of the instability of credit. There is the same need that international credit should be managed, in order to be secure.

We do not need, on the international plane, to feel the Keynesian fear, that purely monetary management will be unable to fight depression; on the international plane it is not Depression, in the old sense, that is the danger. National governments, taught by Keynes, however indirectly, can see to that. What is liable to happen, if there is a failure of international credit, is that nations will turn in upon themselves, becoming more autarkic or more protectionist, impoverishing themselves and each other by refusing to trade with each other. (And this means, we can already see, refusing to *aid* each other.) That is the danger with which we are confronted; we can already see that it is no imaginary danger at this present time.

The remedy, my old nineteenth-century experience would tell us, would be an International Central Bank, an International Bank which would underpin the credit structure, but in order to underpin it must have some control over it. That was what Keynes, who understood this international aspect very clearly, wanted to get at Bretton Woods; but all he got was a Currency Board (for it is little more than a Currency Board, being so tied up with rules and regulations) —the IMF. That, we are finding—and Mill could have told us, one hundred and twenty years ago, that it is what we should find—is not enough. But how should the powers, which governments have been unwilling to entrust to their own Central Banks (once they have realized what is involved) be entrusted to an International Bank? That is the dilemma, the old dilemma, to which we have now come back, on the international plane.

Stated like that, the problem looks insoluble. In such black and white terms, it probably is. But to set rules against no rules is to make too sharp an opposition. Can we find rules that are acceptable to national pride, and to national self-interest, and which yet give scope for some minimum of management—just enough to give the international credit structure the security it so sorely needs? It will be a narrow passage, but one must hope that there will be a way through.

10

THORNTON'S *PAPER CREDIT* (1802)

WHEN *Paper Credit* was reprinted[1] in 1939, it was furnished with an introduction—in most ways an admirable introduction—by Professor Hayek. Most of the things which should be said about Henry Thornton, his life and work, were said by Hayek; they do not need to be repeated. But there was one thing that Hayek did not say. It is not an unimportant thing; to many modern readers it would be the most interesting thing about Thornton. It is the purpose of the present essay to fill the gap.

To Hayek (who considered him especially in his capacity as one of the authors of the Bullion Report), Thornton was one of the fathers of the 'classical' tradition of monetary theory; that he can be considered in that aspect is not to be denied. It will, however, be my contention that there is another aspect to his work, an aspect which makes it far more relevant to modern controversy. Though he came, in the end, to 'classical' conclusions, the route by which he reached them was by no means such as Keynes would have called 'classical'. It incorporated some of the chief things which Keynes, 130 years later, was to rediscover. That it is possible to begin from such premises and yet to reach such conclusions is a lesson that, even now, is worth learning. Whether or not we ourselves would follow the same route—whether or not we can bring ourselves to feel that in Thornton's own day it was a right route—it widens the mind to discover that it was a route which a man of exceptional insight thought it right to follow.

Paper Credit is not, in form, a theoretical book; it contains

[1] In the series 'Library of Economics' published by Allen and Unwin. All references are to this edition.

no model-building, such as we find in Ricardo. It is in part a description of the British monetary system, as it was when Thornton was writing. From that description there are distilled some (very practical) principles; these are illustrated, and evidently influenced, by important events in recent experience. It is impossible to appreciate what Thornton was doing unless it is placed in its historical context. I must say a word about that context, though I shall keep what I have to say extremely brief.

The relevant history is that of the ten years before 1802. The outbreak of war (in February 1793) had caught the British economy at the peak of a period of prosperity, at the crest of a boom which may already have shown signs of faltering. There was a financial panic, marked (so Thornton considered, and the point does not seem to be disputed)[1] by an 'internal drain' of gold from the Bank of England into domestic hoards. The panic was allayed by an issue of Exchequer bills, providing an alternative liquid asset; Thornton is careful to note that the mere promise that the bills would be made available, before any bills were actually issued, was sufficient to quieten nerves. In the following years there were repeated balance-of-payments difficulties, culminating in the major crisis of 1797. Though the immediate cause of that crisis seems to have been a renewed internal drain, the external difficulties which preceded it must have had much to do with the loss of confidence. This was Thornton's view, and (again) it does not seem to be disputed. It was this 1797 crisis which led to the suspension of gold payments by the Bank—the Bank Restriction—as a result of which the bank-note became inconvertible, from 1797 until 1821, after Thornton's death in 1815. The years that followed the Restriction (especially 1799 and 1800) were marked by renewed external pressure; it was the situation of these years

[1] For this historical background, I draw upon Hayek's Introduction; also upon the essay 'Duties of a Banker' by J. K. Horsefield, in Ashton and Sayers, *Papers in English Monetary History*, esp. pp. 23–29; and upon T. S. Ashton, *Economic Fluctuations in England, 1700–1800*, pp. 132–6.

with which Thornton, when writing his book, was most immediately and directly concerned.

He begins, however, by laying some foundations. The first thing to be explained (and for how many decades longer it needed to be explained!) was the place of 'paper credit' (notes and bills) in the asset-liability structure of the whole economy: the relation of the debt structure to the real goods (the economist's 'capital') which appear, together with the debts and credits, in the balance-sheet of each concern. One of the first things which strikes one about Thornton is the clarity of his balance-sheet thinking. It was based, no doubt, upon his experience as a banker; but not all bankers have the imagination to carry their balance-sheet thinking right through their vision of the whole economy, as Thornton (already) did.

From this he proceeds (already in Chapter III) to the velocity of circulation, and the dependence of that on the willingness to hold money. Bills, he is concerned to emphasize, circulate less rapidly than notes, *because they bear interest*. But the extent to which a given rate of interest will tempt people out of cash depends on confidence. This is how he puts it:

The causes which lead to a variation in the rapidity of the circulation of bank notes may be several. In general, it may be observed, that a high state of confidence serves to quicken their circulation; and this happens upon a principle that shall be fully explained. (It must be premised, that by the phrase a more or less quick circulation of notes will be meant a more or less quick circulation of the whole of them on an average. Whatever encreases that reserve, for instance, of Bank of England notes which remains in the drawer of the London banker as his provision against contingencies, contributes to what will here be termed the less quick circulation of the whole.) Now a high state of confidence contributes to make men provide less amply against contingencies. At such a time, they trust, that if the demand upon them for a payment, which is now doubtful and contingent, should actually be made, they shall be able to provide for it at the moment; and they are loth to be at the expence of selling an article, or of getting a bill discounted, in order to make provision much before the period at which it shall be wanted. When, on the contrary, a season of distrust arises, prudence suggests that the loss of interest arising from a detention of notes for a few additional days should not be regarded.[1]

It is not, I think, too much to claim, simply from this passage (and it is not an incidental passage, it is a keystone of Thornton's argument) that he was quite clearly thinking in terms of what Keynes has taught us to call Liquidity Preference. It is Keynes's precautionary motive that he has in mind, not Keynes's speculative motive; but post-Keynesian analysis has made it evident that it is the precautionary motive which is the basis of the voluntary demand for money; Thornton is already beginning to think of operating upon the 'Liquidity Spectrum'. (And notice that for Thornton it is not only the margin between notes and bills that is relevant; 'selling an article' is another alternative that is considered.) All in all, there is as much Liquidity Preference in this passage as anyone could have got—as anyone ought to have got—in 1802.

If we look at these introductory chapters alone (and shut our minds, for the moment, to what was to happen later in the book) we must, I think, be of opinion that Thornton has started off on what we should consider a remarkably Keynesian tack. And it is not in this section alone that he exhibits his 'Keynesianism'; it persists, as we shall see, into the next round.

Chapters IV and V, which purport to be about the Bank of England and the Balance of Payments, are in fact, for the most part, an analysis of the 1797 crisis and of the events which followed from it. He continues in these chapters upon his 'Keynesian' course.

It is in Chapter IV that we find the famous passage on wages, which I shall quote in a moment. Something, however, must first be said about the context of that passage, which is remarkable. Thornton is arguing (in a very modern manner)

---

[1] Thornton, pp. 96–97.

N

against the use of deflation for the rectification of an adverse balance of payments.[1] His argument is deficient because of his lack of a multiplier theory (in this respect, it must be admitted, he falls seriously short of Keynes); but that there will be some reaction, of the kind that Keynes was to analyse by means of the multiplier, he undoubtedly perceives.

That a certain degree of pressure will urge the British merchants in general who buy of the manufacturers, as well as the manufacturers themselves, to sell their goods in order to raise money; that it will thus have some influence in lowering prices at home; and that the low prices at home may tempt merchants to export their articles in the hope of a better price abroad, is by no means an unreasonable supposition. But, then, it is to be observed on the other hand, first, that this more than ordinary eagerness of all our traders to sell, which seems so desirable, is necessarily coupled with a general reluctance to buy, which is proportional to it; it must be obvious, that, when the general body of merchants, being urged by the pecuniary difficulties of the time, are selling their goods in order to raise money, they will naturally also delay making the accustomed purchases of the manufacturer. . . . Thus the manufacturer, on account of the unusual scarcity of money, may even, though the selling price of his article should be profitable, be absolutely compelled by necessity to slacken, if not to suspend, his operations. To inflict such a pressure on the mercantile world as necessarily causes an intermission of manufacturing labour, is obviously not the way to increase that exportable produce, by the excess of which, above the imported articles, gold is to be brought into the country.[2]

It is upon this that the passage on wages follows.

But, secondly, that very diminution in the *price* of manufactures which is supposed to cause them to be exported, may also, if carried very far, produce a suspension of the labour of those

---

[1] It is curious to find Hayek saying (Introduction, p. 39): 'it took some years more for the Bank of England to learn that the way to meet such an internal drain was to grant credits liberally, and then, in learning that lesson, *it forgot that in the case of an external drain exactly the opposite measures were called for.*' This, we know, is (or was) Hayek's view; but it is not at all what Thornton said.

[2] Thornton, pp. 117–18.

who fabricate them. The masters naturally turn off their hands when they find their article selling exceedingly ill. It is true, that if we could suppose the diminution of bank paper to produce permanently a diminution in the value of all articles whatsoever, and a diminution, as it would then be fair that it should do, in the rate of wages also, the encouragement to future manufactures would be the same, though there would be a loss on the stock in hand. The tendency, however, of a very great and sudden re-duction of the accustomed number of bank notes, is to create an *unusual* and *temporary* distress, and a fall of price resulting from that distress. But a fall arising from temporary distress will be attended probably with no correspondent fall in the rate of wages; for the fall of price, and the distress, will be understood to be temporary, and the rate of wages, we know, is not so variable as the price of goods. There is reason, therefore, to fear that the unnatural and extraordinary low price arising from the sort of distress of which we now speak, would occasion much discouragement of the fabrication of manufactures.[1]

So far, then, he has not one but two of the key-points of the Keynesian system; he has Liquidity Preference and he has the stickiness of wages. The latter, indeed, is not so absolute a downward rigidity as it has become in twentieth-century theory—but this is surely a matter of twentieth-century experience. He has quite as much wage-rigidity as it was realistic, in his day, to assume. These things alone are sufficient for the drawing of Keynesian conclusions; and such conclusions, in Chapter V, Thornton proceeds to draw.

He proceeds, in fact, to defend the Bank Restriction; its imposition in 1797 and its maintenance in the years that immediately followed. He interprets the 1797 crisis, as I have indicated, as being (ultimately if not immediately) a consequence of balance-of-payments pressure; itself attri-buted to the obstacles to trade due to war, though it was to be subsequently intensified by harvest failures in 1799 and 1800. Whether this interpretation was correct, is a matter for historians; all that matters to the economist is that this was the reading of the situation that Thornton made. For such

[1] Thornton, pp. 118–19.

an emergency, he strongly holds, deflation is not the remedy. The right course, in the first place, was to let gold go; making up for the deficiency in circulation (when notes were exchanged for gold, and gold exported) by an *expansion* of Bank lending. Nor should such a prescription be changed in essentials, when the gold reserve (at that date an exiguous reserve, we must remember) was exhausted. It is better, under such circumstances, to abandon convertibility than to deflate. That, in effect, is what Thornton says in Chapter V.

Still, however, we are only half-way through his book. And it must be freely admitted that the tone of the rest of the book is very different. The theoretical structure is not significantly changed; it is indeed in these later chapters that we find passages on what Keynes was to call the marginal efficiency of capital—its relation to the rate of interest and its dependence on expectations of price-movements[1]— which are parallel to parts of the Keynesian system not so far considered. Here, too, we find Thornton's version of the doctrine of Full Employment.

But, first, it is obvious that the antecedently idle persons to whom we may suppose the new capital to give employ, are limited in number; and that therefore if the encreased issue is indefinite, it will set to work labourers, of whom a part will be drawn from other, and, perhaps, no less useful occupations. It may be inferred from this consideration, that there are some bounds to the benefit which is to be derived from an augmentation of paper; and, also, that a liberal, or, at most, a large encrease of it, will have all the advantageous effects of the most extravagant emission.[2]

Apart, indeed, from his deficiency on the side of multiplier theory (already noticed) all the significant elements of Keynes's theoretical structure have their echoes in Thornton. But whereas in the first part of the book, the deductions that are drawn are Keynesian; in the second part they are not. What makes the difference?

[1] Thornton, pp. 253–6. See also the passage on pp. 335–6 (from one of the speeches in the Bullion debate).
[2] Thornton, p. 236.

One of the differences, it is clear, is a change in the character of the historical situation that is being considered. One can hardly doubt that the book was written over a considerable period; successive stages of its argument are given topical illustrations, which follow in the book in their right historical order. The psychological elements in velocity of circulation (Chapter III) are illustrated by reference to the 1793 crisis; Chapters IV and V (as we have seen) relate to 1797–1800; the second half of the book (written, one would guess, not long before publication) is looking forward. At that time the harvest crisis appears to be over; and the war itself appears to be over. The Peace of Amiens was signed in March 1802, almost the date of publication; Thornton was not to know that it was a mere armistice, and that hostilities would be so soon resumed. The time had therefore come to show the other side of the medal; the danger of maintaining inconvertibility when it was not necessary.

Thornton had observed that exchange depreciation can occur (under inconvertibility) without over-issue; but he is not inclined to deny that inconvertibility facilitates over-issue; and he is strongly convinced that over-issue (or, as we should say, inflation) is dangerous and deplorable. So he moves his guns to the other side of the ship. He allows that expansion in the supply of money sets idle hands to work; but it cannot do much in that direction without raising prices.

Let us also consider the mode in which the new paper operates through the medium of these individual borrowers, as unquestionably it does, in giving life to fresh industry. The bank notes convey to them the power of obtaining for their own use, or of destining to such purposes as they please, a certain portion of purchasable commodities. The extraordinary emission of paper causes no immediate difference in the *total* quantity of articles belonging to the kingdom. This is self-evident. But it communicates to the new borrowers at the bank a power of taking to themselves a larger share of the existing goods than they would otherwise have been able to command. If the holders of the new paper thus acquire the power over a larger portion of the existing stock of the kingdom, the possessors of the old paper must have the power over a smaller part. The same paper, therefore, will purchase fewer goods, or, in other words, commodities will rise in their nominal value. . . .

It may be said, however, and not untruly, that an encreased issue of paper tends to produce a more brisk demand for the existing goods, and a somewhat more prompt consumption of them; that the more prompt consumption supposes a diminution of the ordinary stock, and the application of that part of it, which is consumed, to the purpose of giving life to fresh industry; that the fresh industry thus excited will be the means of gradually creating additional stock, which will serve to replace the stock by which industry had been supported; and that the new circulating medium will, in this manner, create for itself much new employment.[1]

The supposition which has now been made is admitted to be just. Let the reader, however, take notice, that it assumes the demand both for goods and labour to become more eager than before. Now the consequence of this encreased demand must, unquestionably, be an enhancement of the price of labour and commodities, which is the very point for which I am contending.[2]

Taken in conjunction with the passage about Full Employment which I have quoted (they appear, in fact, next door to one another) we are justified, I think, in summarizing Thornton's view in the statement that while wages are rigid against temporary changes in the demand for labour, against permanent changes (or changes that look like being permanent) they are not.

Under inconvertibility, there is a danger of inflation; a danger which is enhanced, in Thornton's day (and the point is emphasized by Thornton's own principles) by the 5 per cent. maximum on the lending rate of the Bank.[3] It is therefore essential that the Bank should keep a firm hand on the circulation; and the need for controlling the issue of Bank

---

[1] That is to say, in the (limited) Keynesian sense, 'equilibrium' will be restored.

[2] Thornton, pp. 236–7.   [3] Thornton, p. 254.

notes is emphasized in a way that brings Thornton very near to Ricardo.

It was doubtless this change in emphasis (underlined by Thornton's subsequent membership of the Bullion Committee, and general adherence to its doctrines) which accounts for the subsequent decline in Thornton's influence. It was natural for people to get the impression that Thornton was saying more or less the same thing as Ricardo, and the later authority (who had in mind a later situation) eclipsed the earlier. But it may be that there is one particular aspect of the discussion in Thornton's later chapters which was particularly responsible for his doctrine being confounded with Ricardo's. Like Ricardo, he maintains (or seems to maintain) that *the* test of over-issue (or of inflation) is a fall in the exchange: in his terminology, an excess of the market price of bullion over the mint price.

It is the maintenance of the general exchanges, or, in other words, it is the agreement of the mint price with the bullion price of gold which seems to be the true proof that the circulating paper is not depreciated.[1]

Though he qualifies it later,[2] he does make this statement, and makes it in a conspicuous place. From Thornton, it is an extraordinary statement. He had previously shown, in his analysis of the 1797 crisis, that the exchange might fall, without any expansion of issue by the Bank, and without there being any case (in his view) for a contraction of issue. How could he square these two pronouncements?

The first line of defence (or explanation) which occurs to one is the following. Thornton was confronted with a difficulty in prescribing a test for inflation. He was quite firm that mere increase in the note issue was no adequate test. He had shown, and emphasized, that occasions must arise when the note issue ought to be expanded to meet a rise in the demand for money (an increase in Liquidity Preference) or to offset a fall in the supply of other sorts of money. That

[1] Thornton, p. 192.   [2] Thornton, p. 261.

test was therefore unacceptable. But if it was abandoned, what was the alternative? Index-numbers, of prices (and of course still more of quantities) were more than half a century in the future. What alternative, other than the price of bullion, did exist?

There may be something in that; but if we offer Thornton an excuse on those lines, does it not equally apply to Ricardo?

I think that there is another defence—deeper and more subtle. If the passage which I have just quoted is read in the context of the whole book, one can guess what it is that Thornton really meant.

It must first be emphasized that Thornton always believed in the Gold Standard. That looks a surprising statement, in view of his support of the 1797 Restriction; but I believe it is true. Certainly no more uncompromising statement of that adherence can be found than in the quotation which he makes in one of his speeches in the House of Commons:

It might be true that to the King, generally speaking, was committed the regulation of the coin of a country; but the language he should be disposed to use, would be that, not of his Right Honourable Friend,[1] but rather of Sir Thomas Rowe, at the Council table of Charles I;—a language, indeed, in the first words of it a little resembling the Resolution on which he was animadverting, but far different in its conclusion. 'The regulating of coin' said Sir T. Rowe, 'hath been left to the care of princes, who have ever been presumed to be the fathers of the commonwealth. *Upon their honours they are debtors and warrantees of justice to the subject in that behalf.*'[2]

This, to be sure, is 1811, not 1802; but it is incredible that the man who believed this, with such conviction, in 1811 could ever have believed anything else.

In the light of this, the defence of the 1797 Restriction must be looked at again.

The monetary circulation, as it was in 1797, consisted of gold coin (guineas) as well as of Bank of England notes— putting on one side the token coin and country bank-notes,

---

[1] Chancellor of the Exchequer Vansittart.   [2] Thornton, p. 360.

with which we are not here concerned. When the Bank suspended gold payments, the bank-notes fell in value relatively to gold bullion. But what happened to the gold coin? Thornton is careful to explain[1] that the coin remained at par with the notes, both remaining equally acceptable. But that implied that there was a fall in the value of coin relatively to bullion; a profit was therefore to be gained from melting down the coin and exporting it. This was illegal, but it happened. Thus the process of melting and exporting provided a new and acceptable export, which filled the gap in the Balance of Payments and prevented the exchange from falling very far. In fact, up to the point when 'Paper Credit' was written in 1802 the exchange had only fallen about 10 per cent.; this was sufficient to cause the gold to come out of circulation and to be exported. (There was an increase in the bank-note issue to supply the place of the lost gold; this increase Thornton defends.)

The function of the 10 per cent. depreciation was to mobilize the secondary gold reserve—the gold coin in circulation. In order to meet a temporary difficulty, this depreciation was entirely justifiable. If it was only done to meet a temporary difficulty, it did not (in Thornton's view) imply any definitive abandonment of the Gold Standard. It was simply a matter of 'widening the gold points' such as Keynes was to recommend in the nineteen-twenties. A depreciation to that extent did no more than impart a useful flexibility to the Gold Standard mechanism. Such flexibility Thornton approves.

What, however, was to happen if the emergency persisted, until all the gold, that could readily be drawn out of circulation, had gone? There would then, if expansion continued, be a further depreciation; it is this further depreciation which (I think) Thornton has in mind when he speaks of exchange depreciation measuring true over-issue. Though there would still be gold coin in the country, it would not, to any important extent, be circulating. It would be held as a speculative counter, waiting the day when (legally or illegally)

[1] Thornton, pp. 148–50.

it could be changed into notes at a more advantageous rate. This would be the point (it would inevitably be a matter of judgement just when this point was reached) when the Gold Standard, as Thornton conceived it, would in effect be abandoned. Against abandonment, in that sense, Thornton always set his face.

On this interpretation, Thornton emerges as a very consistent thinker. But his consistency depends upon his belief that it is possible to draw a firm line between what is appropriate in short-run temporary emergencies, and what is appropriate for long-run permanent policy. For the short-run, he is Keynesian; far more consistently Keynesian than the muddled Malthus. Yet Keynes could never have taken Thornton for a mascot, as he did Malthus; for when it comes to the long-run, Thornton is the hardest of hard-money men. He is every bit as hard as Ricardo. Like Ricardo, he would have fought against devaluation, when the emergency (even though short-run had passed into long-run for more than a decade) was finally over. In fact, he was dead before that issue had to be faced; but it cannot be doubted, from the evidence of his contributions to the Bullion debates, that he would have stood for a restoration of the old parity. Like Ricardo (but for different reasons than Ricardo's)[1] he would have desired that the restoration should be managed more skilfully, and more gently, than it was; but that is as far as one can see him going.

These, however, are historical questions; and the present (as will be only too obvious) is not a historical essay. *Paper Credit* is much more than the tract for the times that it appears on the surface. Strip it of its topicalities, and of the empirical assumptions, which may or may not have been appropriate in Thornton's own day, it remains a work of permanent value. Thornton is in the front rank of monetary economists; he is the peer of those that we have seen in our

---

[1] Ricardo's views on resumption are discussed by Sayers, in *Papers in English Monetary History*, pp. 83–89. One has a feeling that the Ingot Plan would have been too mechanical a remedy for Thornton.

own time. In his short-run theory, as we have seen, he is very near to Keynes; but if we take both wings together, he is nearer still, perhaps, to Robertson.[1] We can better understand what it was that separated Robertson from Keynes when we bring Thornton in as a standard of reference.

For there is one essential idea of Thornton's, which I have not yet mentioned, but which it will be fitting to emphasize in conclusion. Every economy is liable to unexpected shocks —of which the harvest failures, that are Thornton's principal example, are of course no more than an example. One of the things which we should require of economic organization is that its institutions should be such that it can stand up to shocks; that it should have cushions against them, so that their secondary repercussions are minimized, not intensified by the fears and alarms that they so easily engender. But there are few cushions that will drop into place automatically; the most that is usually possible is that there should be reserves which can be used, if there are people who have the courage and skill to use them, at the right and not at the wrong time. A developed credit system—in which notes and bills and trade credits (and the bank deposits which were to come) are used in part substitute for hard money—has the advantage over a pure hard money system, in that its reserves are in places where they can more readily be used, if there is the intelligence and strength of will to use them. It is, of course, only too true that these essential qualities may not be there. But to fall back on rules, making the monetary system mechanical, is a confession of failure. Thornton, we may be sure, would not have approved of Fiduciary Issues, or Reserve Ratios; he was setting his sights higher than that.

From that point of view, his hardness—his long-run hardness—readily fits in. Reserves will be more confidently used (and not over-used) as short-run stabilizers, if confidence in

---

[1] Robertson knew that this was so, though I suspect that he did not read Thornton until the reprint appeared in 1939. I remember telling him that I was preparing the lecture, of which the present paper is an elaboration. 'Oh, Thornton,' he said 'he knew everything.' They were indeed very close together.

long-run stability is unimpaired. Here, of course, in relation to modern attitudes, comes the great divide. Once it is assumed that money wages are always inflexible downwards, even in the long-run, the stability on which Thornton reckoned is inevitably gone. But was it the abandonment of long-run price-stability, or the wage-inflexibility, which came first? If we were reporting to Thornton what has happened since his time, that is one of the questions which we should have to answer.

11

A NOTE ON THE *TREATISE*

1. WE have found ourselves, at several points in the preceding Essays, coming back to the *Treatise on Money*.
'Keynes', to the modern student, means the *General Theory*
(or, only too probably, some exposition of the *General
Theory*); the categories of the *General Theory* are those in
which he has learned to think. But the *General Theory* is not
all of Keynes. There is much of Keynes's earlier work that is
absorbed into it, but there is much of permanent value which
is not so absorbed. To take the most obvious example: the
General Theory is the theory of a closed economy. If we want
to read what Keynes said on the theory of international money
(not just what other people think he ought to have said), we
have to go to the *Treatise*. Even intra-national monetary theory
is much more fully developed in the *Treatise* than in the later
work. Money, in the *General Theory*, is stripped to its bare
bones; we get no more of the monetary system than is
absolutely necessary for a particular purpose. The *Treatise*
is a Treatise on Money, in a way that the other is not.

It is highly desirable, for these reasons, and there are others
as well, that the *Treatise* should be brought back into circulation.[1] But the modern student (including in that description
nearly all those who have learned their economics since,
say, 1940) can hardly be expected to go to the *Treatise*, and
draw from it what he ought to draw from it, unless he is
given a little help. It is bound to look, at a first impression,
like a work written in a foreign language. One has to learn
the language before one can read it.

The terminology, of course, has always been a bother. And

[1] I am glad to see that Sir Roy Harrod takes the same view. See his
review of Kaldor's *Essays on Economic Policy* (*EJ*, Dec. 1965, p. 798).

Keynes does try to explain it (Chapter 9). But the explanation is directed towards the readers he could expect in 1930; even for them, as experience proved, it was not a wholly adequate explanation. What the modern reader requires is something different, since he is approaching the matter from the other end. He has been brought up on the late Keynesian, or post-Keynesian, terminology; the early Keynesian terminology of the *Treatise* must offer for him a different kind of difficulty from that which its original readers could possibly have felt. What I hope to do in this note is to give some help with this new kind of difficulty.

2. The crucial chapters are Chapter 9, 'Certain Definitions' and Chapter 10, the 'Fundamental Equations'. There is little in Chapters 1–8 which need cause trouble; little, indeed, which is necessary nowadays for an understanding of what is to follow. The classification of Bank Deposits (p. 34) needs to be noticed. It is not the same as the famous 'Triad' of the *General Theory*; but it is tending that way, and will be further elaborated in the direction of the Triad in Chapter 15. Chapters 4–8, on the 'Value of Money', contain much matter on index-numbers which we would not now expect to find in a monetary treatise. Their chief purpose is to emphasize the importance of sectional price-levels, as against the 'general' price-level, with which monetary theory had formerly been mainly concerned. This is a lesson which has now so thoroughly sunk in as to be a bit boring. All that requires to be noticed, for the purposes of later chapters, is the rather tiresome trick of vocabulary that is carried over from these discussions: the habit of referring to these sectoral price-levels as 'standards'—Consumption Standard, Labour Standard, and so on. The reader must just learn to translate.

3. So we come to Chapter 9, where the fun starts. Before commenting on the Definitions in detail, there are two general points that need to be made.

The first is to emphasize that the Social Accounting schema of National Income and Expenditure, which the modern student takes almost at the beginning of his studies in

economics, was in 1930 quite unavailable. It is itself one of
the things which has emerged from Keynes's work (though
there are many others than Keynes who have played a part
in its construction). Even at the *General Theory* stage it
remained unfinished, but the schema that is used there is
near enough to that which has become orthodox to give no
substantial trouble.[1] It is far otherwise in the *Treatise*. Critical
words, like 'income', 'earnings', 'profits', and 'saving', are
used in the *Treatise* in senses far different from those which
have become familiar. We do indeed have to realize that
these accounting terms are being used for concepts which
are not accounting concepts. Though the 'Fundamental
Equations' look like accounting identities, the terms of which
they are composed are economic-theoretical, not accounting
categories; that is why they can be used in a way in which
accounting identities could not be used. The schema of the
Treatise will in time give birth to Social Accounting, but it is
not yet Social Accounting; it is much safer to regard it as a
theoretical model.

Even as a model (and this is my second point) it needs to
be placed in a context that is not fully explained. Keynes, I
think, is contemplating a process of expansion (we had
better not say monetary expansion, since that sounds as if
the quantity of money must be involved, as he is anxious to
insist it need not be) as taking place in three stages. In
Stage One there is a rise in *flexible* prices (of capital goods
or of consumer goods) without any change in output or in
employment. In Stage Two comes the change in *real*
activity (employment and output). In Stage Three comes the
rise in *rigid* prices (wages and so on). Of course, it is not
maintained that every particular expansion will last long
enough to work through to Stage Three; it may peter out
before it gets there.

Put in these terms, there is nothing very original about the
model; Hume, as I have indicated elsewhere,[2] had put

---

[1] For Keynes's last work on Social Accounting, see the Appendix to
his *How to Pay for the War* (1940).   [2] Above, p. 161.

forward something very like it (as a model of *monetary* expansion) almost two hundred years before. The peculiarity of the treatment in the *Treatise* is the extreme concentration on what I have called Stage One. Stages Two and Three are there; they make their appearance, time and time again, in the verbal discussion. But it is Stage One alone that is closely analysed; it is Stage One alone to which the Fundamental Equations essentially refer.

This is odd; and it seems even odder now than it did in 1930. For in the *General Theory* it was Stage Two that was to become the focus of attention; Stage One took a back seat. Later on, in the post-Keynesian epoch, the movement of prices, in direct response to effective demand, has been played down even more than it was in the *General Theory*. We tend now to think of all prices (excepting, perhaps, the prices of securities and some raw materials) as being *more or less* rigid, rigid (that is to say) against demand pressure. In a world of this character, Stages One and Two, as I have numbered them, will have changed places. What is left of Stage One can then be subsumed under Stage Three—it being granted, of course, that some prices will be more rigid than others.

Which of these orderings is right is an empirical question; it is entirely possible that there may have been some times and places for which the one ordering is the more suitable, some for which it is the other. But it is not really to be supposed that there was so marked a change in economic structure between 1930 and 1936 (in England or in America) that the *Treatise* arrangement can have been right at its own date while only six years later there was a complete changeover. My own guess would be that the *Treatise* ordering was not deliberately selected to fit what were supposed to be the facts of 1930. Keynes was writing a Treatise on Money, and this appeared to be a non-monetary matter. He did not feel it incumbent on him to examine it directly. He just took over what he had learned from Marshall.

In Marshall, as I have explained in another place,[1] 'firms

[1] *Capital and Growth*, p. 55.

are not price-makers, as we have learned to think firms to be when they operate in an imperfect market. Prices are not set by firms and then altered if they turn out to be wrong. They are more flexible than that; so they can be *determined* by demand and supply, by the bargaining of the market.' So it is, usually at least, in the *Treatise*. For the conditions of Marshall's day, his assumption can I think be defended; for the standardized and branded goods which are so well fitted for (official or unofficial) retail price maintenance had then scarcely appeared. In Marshall's day 'an increase in demand would not be allowed to remain unsatisfied or to run down stocks unduly. Prices would rise, not because of any action by the manufacturer, nor indeed by the ultimate consumer (who, then as now, would normally be a passive party); the initiative would come from the wholesaler or shopkeeper, who would offer higher prices to get the goods which even at the higher price he could sell at a profit'.[1] This was Marshall's world; it was this world that Keynes (in 1930) was implicitly assuming. Whether it was *really* the world of 1930 seems to me very doubtful. In any case, by 1936 he had come to reject it.

I make no question that in 1936 he was right to reject it. But that does not mean that we should also be right to reject it in our day: that therefore the *Treatise* model has nothing for us *now*. Surely it has come back into its own in another way. The *Treatise* model can still be used for the analysis of demand inflation—for the analysis of the effects of an expansion of demand that begins from Full Employment, from a condition in which the economy is already producing to capacity, so that a further rise in real activity (Stage Two) is ruled out, or largely ruled out. Even in such a condition it will still be the case that some prices are more rigid than others. There may still be a lag of wages behind prices, and to that phase the *Treatise* analysis will apply. I am not suggesting that we have come to a point where we can leave the *General Theory* ordering and go back to the old ordering, only that there is room for both.

[1] Ibid., pp. 55–56.

4. We are now in a position to come to the details of the 'Definitions' and of the 'Fundamental Equations'. We can now see that we are to regard them as a formal analysis of Stage One.

In Stage One, the rigid prices (wages and so on) are to be taken as fixed. The system is defined to be in *equilibrium* so long as the flexible prices are *in line with* the rigid prices. But what is that to mean? Keynes, we can see, has some doubts about it, but he plumps for saying that the flexible prices are to be such as to leave *entrepreneurs* (in general) with no more and no less than their *normal* remuneration, defined (p. 125) as 'that rate of remuneration which, if they were open to make new bargains with the factors of production at the currently prevailing rates of earnings, would leave them under no motive to increase or to decrease their scale of operations'. Their scale of operations, one must suppose, whatever that is, for no further restriction is given.[1] Alternatively, one may say that equilibrium prices are equal to costs, costs which include the remuneration of *entrepreneurs*, in the above sense.

When this is understood, Keynes's initial statement (p. 123) that he is going to mean 'identically the same thing by the three expressions: the community's money income, the earnings of the factors of production, and the cost of production' need cause no trouble. We must simply remember that these are income and earnings *in equilibrium*.

In equilibrium, the Social Accounts will come out right, even as we are now accustomed to take them. Income is divided into Consumption and Saving, and Saving must equal the increment of Capital or (net) Investment. Costs and values are the same.

But what interests Keynes is the disequilibrium position, when the flexible prices are not in line. Here it is necessary to take the sectoral price-levels separately.

Let P_1 be the actual (disequilibrium) price-level of

[1] This is a point which was to cause much heart-searching on the way to the *General Theory*. We shall meet it again when we come to the Natural Rate of Interest (below, p. 199).

consumption goods, considered as an index-number *with the equilibrium price-level taken as base.* (Keynes takes an arbitrary base, but there is no reason why we should not take any base that is convenient, and by taking this particular base we get a good deal of simplification.[1]) Let R be the value of consumption at equilibrium prices (what Keynes would call its cost of production). Then, since we are still at Stage One, so that the quantities produced and consumed are supposed to be the same in disequilibrium as in equilibrium, the value of consumption, in disequilibrium, will be $P_1 R$. The difference between $P_1 R$ and R is the 'profit' (in Keynes's special sense) that accrues in the consumption sector. He calls this Q_1.

So
$$P_1 R = R + Q_1.$$

Let P_2 be the disequilibrium price-level of investment goods, similarly measured, and let C be the equilibrium value of the net investment. Then $P_2 C$ is the disequilibrium value of the net investment, and

$$P_2 C = C + Q_2,$$

where Q_2 is the corresponding profit.

If P is the disequilibrium price-level of output as a whole, again similarly measured,

$$P = \frac{P_1 R + P_2 C}{R + C} = 1 + \frac{Q_1 + Q_2}{R + C} = 1 + \frac{Q}{E},$$

where Q is total profit, and E is total 'income', i.e. equilibrium income.[2]

---

[1] Keynes took an arbitrary base, because he wanted to include the effects of spontaneous changes in wage-rates, and spontaneous changes in efficiency (which alter the equilibrium relations between his price-levels) in the same formula. But there would have been no difficulty in dealing with these things separately; there would, I think, have been a gain in clarity if he had done so.

By taking equilibrium prices as base, we can set Keynes's I' equal to his C, and his O equal to his E. Thus we can economize in symbols.

[2] Keynes would write O in the denominator of the last formula, but by our assumption about base, E and O are the same.

All this, so far, is pure definition, or algebra working on definitions. It is at the next step that Keynes introduced 'behavioural' assumptions, so as to convert his system of definitions into a model. By far the most important of these is that the value of investment ($P_2 C$—or, as Keynes writes it, I) is determined independently of the flow magnitudes hitherto considered; so far as they are concerned it is exogenous. This is vital; but since it is an assumption that is (in effect) carried over to the *General Theory*, and will be perfectly familiar to the modern reader, I need not delay over it now, though I must come back to it later.

The other assumption is that the value of consumption ($P_1 R$) depends solely upon saving propensities; it is un-affected by anything else, as for instance P_1 (the price-level of consumption goods). And Keynes clearly holds (p. 148) that it is a good approximation to take it that what matters is the saving-propensity out of income (again meaning equilibrium income); for the 'profits' (Q) that are earned in the current period will not have had time to be distributed (remember that we are still at Stage One) so they will not affect consumption. (Even if they do, it will not matter all that much as we shall see in a moment.) If the possibility of consumption out of profits is neglected,

$$P_1 R = E - s_1 E,$$

where s_1 is the propensity to save out of 'income', or

$$P_1 R = E - S$$

as Keynes would write it. Then, since $P_2 C = I$,

$$P = \frac{P_1 R + P_2 C}{E} = \frac{E - S + I}{E} = 1 + \frac{I - S}{E},$$

which (effectively) is Keynes's *Fundamental Equation*.[1] (It will be noticed that $Q = I - S$.)

Now suppose that there is some consumption out of

---

[1] Strictly speaking, it is Keynes's second Fundamental Equation. His first has already been absorbed.

'profits'. Write the propensity to consume out of profits, analogously, as $1-s_2$. We would then have

$$P_1 R = (1-s_1) E + (1-s_2) Q$$

and $\qquad E+Q = P_1 R + P_2 C = E + Q - s_1 E - s_2 Q + I$

so that $\qquad\qquad\qquad I = s_1 E + s_2 Q$

whence $\qquad\qquad\qquad Q = (I-S)/s_2$

and $\qquad\qquad P = 1 + \dfrac{Q}{E} = 1 + \dfrac{I-S}{s_2 E},$

a revised form of the Fundamental Equation.

Keynes (rather irritatingly) does not give this form of the Fundamental Equation explicitly; he leaves it to be inferred from the rhetorical passage about the Danaid Jar (p. 139) and from many other references. It is much to be wished that it had been written out. For it would then have become clear why it is that saving out of 'income' (S or $s_1 E$) has the special role which it has in the *Treatise* model. If there is no consumption out of profits ($s_2 = 1$), profits are *equal* to the 'gap' between 'saving' and investment; if there is consumption out of profits, profits are equal to the same gap with a multiplier applied to it. (The parallel between this multiplier and the famous Multiplier of the *General Theory* is very instructive. In the form I have just given to it, it is like the 'Keynesian' Multiplier of the *General Theory* in being the final stage of a process—for there can be no consumption out of profits until there are profits! It cries aloud to have a process analysis, like that of the Kahn multiplier, applied to it.)

In 'real' terms—that is to say, if we value throughout at equilibrium prices—consumption is always R, and investment is always C. At current prices, on the other hand, investment is I, which is financed in part by saving out of income (S) and in part by accumulation out of profits ($I-S$). If we are to reduce these to real terms by deflating by a price-index, we must be careful what index we use. The index of investment good prices (P_2) is insensitive to consumption out of profits, since it is equal to I/C, whatever is s_2. The other indexes $(P_1$ and $P)$ are not thus insensitive. If we deflate by P (which is higher when there is consumption out of profits than when there is not), the real value of investment will appear to be reduced below what it would have been otherwise; and the accumulation out of profits will also appear to be lower. These effects will be still more marked if we deflate by P_1. It would accordingly appear that when Keynes, in the Danaid Jar passage, says that 'however much of their profits entrepreneurs spend on consumption, the increment of wealth belonging to entrepreneurs remains the same as before' (p. 139), he is implicitly deflating by P_2. He might, I think, have explained.

5. I return to the Value of Investment (I), or to the price-level of investment goods (P_2), which amounts to the same thing. For we are still at Stage One; $I = P_2 C$, and C is fixed. As I have said, the Value of Investment is determined independently of the flow magnitudes with which we have been hitherto concerned. It is in fact determined in much the same way as the Volume of Investment in the *General Theory*. Names are different, but the characters are readily recognizable. In place of Liquidity Preference (or at least of the Speculative Motive) we have 'excess-bearishness'; in place of the Marginal Efficiency of Capital we have the Natural Rate of Interest.

'Excess-bearishness'—'such excess of bearishness on the part of the public as is unsatisfied by the creation of deposits by the banking system' (p. 144)—will be readily recognized as the forerunner of Liquidity Preference; its action in the determination of the Rate of Interest follows, very broadly, the familiar lines. I shall not attempt to follow this out in detail in this place, since I do not think that it is necessary to do so. Once the clue is given, the reader can go straight ahead. It must just again be emphasized that the analysis is in many ways more subtle than that in the corresponding parts of the General Theory.[1] The strictly monetary chapters of the *Treatise* are some of the best chapters. It is largely in order to assist in opening the door to these chapters (15, 17, 22–26, 31–33, 37) that I am writing this Note. But I do not think that they require any more specific introduction.

It is otherwise with the 'Natural Rate of Interest' on which there are things of great importance that remain to be said.

Since the Value of Investment (I) is taken to depend upon the Rate of Interest—conceived, it must be emphasized, in a wide way, so that it can be rewritten as 'terms of credit', as on p. 183—there should be some Rate of Interest which makes the Value of Investment equal to the Saving[2] that is otherwise determined; the establishment of this Rate of Interest can thus be regarded as a condition of equilibrium, in the sense of the preceding model. It is this rate which is Keynes's Natural Rate. The term, of course, was borrowed from Wicksell; though, as we shall see, it is not used in Wicksell's manner.

In the *General Theory* (p. 242) the Natural Rate of the *Treatise* is explicitly withdrawn. We can see why. It is a part of the general shift of attention, between the two books, from what we have been calling Stage One to what we have been calling Stage Two. As we have seen[3] the equilibrium of the *Treatise* is a condition in which the earnings of *entrepreneurs* are normal, in the sense that 'they have no motive to increase or to decrease their scale of operations'. The economy can be in equilibrium, in this limited sense, even though the scale of operations is far below capacity; for nothing is said about capacity, or about employment, in this definition. There can be equilibrium, in this sense, at the bottom of a slump; with earnings so low that there is no incentive to expansion, so long as there is no further incentive to contraction either. A Natural Rate, which sets a mark for the

---

[1] The *Treatise* and the *General Theory* approaches to money and interest are synthesized, and further developed, in R. F. Kahn, 'Notes on Liquidity Preference' (*Manchester School*, 1954).

[2] 'Saving', it will be remembered, out of 'Income'.

[3] Above, p. 194.

actual rate to attain so that it should have this property, has come by 1936 to seem to Keynes to have little importance.

The point applies, however, not merely to the Natural Rate, but to Stage One analysis in general. If we can find a situation in which we still want to apply Stage One analysis (and I have suggested that in relation to problems of Inflation we may well be able to find it) a Natural Rate, in the *Treatise* sense, can still come back into the picture. But that is by no means all that there is to be said.

Though the Natural Rate of the *Treatise* is taken from Wicksell, it is admitted (p. 197) to be a 'reinterpretation' of Wicksell; and in the reinterpretation much has been lost, as well as something gained. Equilibrium, in Keynes, is always a short-period equilibrium; in the *Treatise*, indeed, it is an ultra-short-period equilibrium; one can, however, be quite confident in asserting that Wicksell was not thinking on those lines. At the time when he wrote the *Treatise*, all of Wicksell that Keynes can have absorbed was *Geldzins und Güterpreise* (*Interest and Prices*); it may well be that in that book the point is not perfectly clear. But in the rest of Wicksell's work (now for the most part readily available in English) it is overwhelmingly apparent. He came to the doctrine of *Interest and Prices* from his work in non-monetary economics, especially from his study of the conditions for the long-period stationary equilibrium of a closed economy, taken in real terms. When he turned to apply his doctrine to empirical reality, it was a long-period problem (the downward trend of the wholesale price-level between 1870 and 1895) that he selected.[1]

There is in Wicksell no sharp opposition between rigid and flexible prices, as there is in the *Treatise*. For his long-period purpose, all prices are flexible, though some (no doubt he could admit) may be more flexible than others. Thus in Wicksell a slump condition of acute unemployment

[1] See his paper 'The Influence of the Rate of Interest on Commodity Prices' (1899), translated in his *Selected Papers on Economic Theory*.

could not be an equilibrium (as Keynes found himself saying it would be, from strict application of the *Treatise* definition); for one of the conditions of long-period equilibrium, as Wicksell would see it, would not be satisfied, the level of money wages having a tendency to fall. So the strictures which Keynes makes in the *General Theory* on the Natural Rate of the *Treatise* do not apply to the Natural Rate of Wicksell. Wicksellian analysis and Keynesian are not the same. There is a place for each of them.[1]

I am by no means implying that Wicksell himself said the last word in the elaboration of his own ideas. There was much which he left to be done, but it was not Keynes who did it. It will be fitting to conclude with a reference to two works that are contemporary with Keynes's (they appeared indeed between the *Treatise* and the *General Theory*) and which seem to me to be much more genuinely Wicksellian, marking important advances in the application of a Wicksellian method. One of them is Myrdal's *Monetary Equilibrium*.[2] Here the Wicksellian construction is re-thought in terms of sectional price-levels; distinction is made between the Natural Rates that are appropriate for the stabilization of different price-levels, stabilization of the consumption price-level (P_1) of the investment good price-level (P_2) and of the wage-level being recognized to be different things. Preference is finally given for a stabilization (in the Wicksellian sense, which involves at least approximate demand-supply equalization) of the relatively rigid prices, that is to say, of the wage-level or of the stickier part of the wage-level. This is a route which was open to a Wicksellian, even after

[1] The paths are distinct, but they may cross. Thus one may read Keynes's Chapter 21, on International Disequilibrium, with the Natural Rate interpreted strictly in the *Treatise* sense, and so (as we have seen) taking it to refer to the transmission of inflation between fully employed economies. But it does not need much amendment if it is to be read as referring to longer periods, in which case we can shift our interpretation of the Natural Rate in a Wicksellian direction.

[2] This was published in Swedish in 1931, in German (as one of the essays in *Beiträge zur Geldtheorie*, edited by Hayek) in 1933, and in English in 1939. See my review of the German version in *Economica*, Dec. 1934.

he had read and absorbed the *Treatise*; but it is, of course, not the route which Keynes himself took.

The other is Dennis Robertson's paper *Industrial Fluctuation and the Natural Rate of Interest*,[1] a paper which may be criticized in detail, but which seems to me to be on the whole one of his important works. The Natural Rate, in Robertson, is not the Natural Rate of the *Treatise*; it is much nearer to Wicksell's than Keynes's was. It is essentially a property of the norm about which fluctuations occur. Robertson is working back from the long-period, which was Wicksell's concern—and forward from the short-period, which was always so much the concern of Keynes—towards a middle-period analysis, which he held to be the appropriate method for the study of fluctuations. This, it must be remembered, had always been Robertson's special subject, from his early *Study in Industrial Fluctuation* (1915) onwards. He was always much preoccupied with the *real* causes of fluctuation. His study of those causes had convinced him that not all fluctuation was undesirable, or 'inappropriate'.[2] Some reserve of resources (labour, and other resources than labour) is needed in order that an economy should be able to cope with the unexpected demands which must always be expected to be made upon it. It is quite wrong that people should have to suffer in order to provide this reserve; it is a fault in organization when they are made to do so. But to 'provide work' in order to keep this desirable reserve 'fully employed' is as wrong as to provide crime in order to ensure the full employment of policemen. The point is surely valid, though there may be differences of opinion about its importance. Keynes took one view, Robertson the other. It must always be remembered, when reading Robertson, that he is approaching the questions at issue from this angle; and when reading Keynes on Robertson, as in Chapter 19 of the *Treatise*.

[1] *EJ*, Dec. 1934. It is reprinted in his *Essays in Monetary Theory* and in the paperback collection, *Essays in Money and Interest*.
[2] *Banking Policy and the Price Level*, ch. 3.

12

THE HAYEK STORY

I

WHEN the definitive history of economic analysis during the nineteen-thirties comes to be written, a leading character in the drama (it was quite a drama) will be Professor Hayek. Hayek's economic writings—I am not concerned with his later work in political theory and in sociology—are almost unknown to the modern student; it is hardly remembered that there was a time when the new theories of Hayek were the principal rival of the new theories of Keynes. Which was right, Keynes or Hayek? There are many still living teachers of economics, and practical economists, who have passed through a time when they had to make up their minds on that question; and there are many of them (including the present writer) who took quite a time to make up their minds. How was it that this happened? It is, at the least, an interesting historical question; and it may be more. If a theory (a rather complex theory) is to have even a temporary success, there must be something about it that rings a bell. That the immediate impact of the Hayek theory was extremely misleading is not now to be questioned; yet some of the issues to which it drew attention were real issues, issues that economists have found it hard to understand and which perhaps even now have not been completely cleared up.

It will be well to begin with some chronology. Hayek's *Prices and Production* was published in September 1931, but the lectures on which it was based had been given in London the previous February; Keynes's *Treatise on Money* was published in December 1930. It may thus be said that the two works came into the world at almost exactly the same time; and it was a time—just when the full dimensions of the World Slump were declaring themselves—at which the need for some new knowledge on the subject of Fluctuations was exceptionally high. Each of the authors had been working on the subject for years, but there had been hardly any contact between them. There is, indeed, in Keynes's book a curious passage[1] in which he seeks support for his own innovations in the work that was being done, by Hayek and others, in Vienna; but the publications mentioned are all in German, and it is clear that Keynes had not studied them closely. For it was only too obvious, when the books were available for comparison, that Keynes and Hayek were not saying the same thing. The practical conclusions which they reached clashed far too violently.

What was in common between them—all that seemed to be in common between them—was the intellectual descent which each claimed from Wicksell; but Wicksell plus Keynes said one thing, Wicksell plus Hayek said quite another. Which was right? It must be insisted, in defence of those who got so puzzled in 1931–3, that no more was yet available to them, on Keynes's side, than what was in the *Treatise*; stimulating ideas which, on their author's own admission, still needed a lot of sorting out. The pattern of Hayek's thought, at a first impression, looked more coherent. The obstacle which confronted one on his side was his Böhm–Bawerkian model; an analytical framework that had become familiar, even orthodox, in some continental countries, but was unfamiliar in England. *Prices and Production* was in English, but it was not English economics. It needed further translation before it could be properly assessed.

Several of us made attempts at that translation; the journals of the nineteen-thirties are full of them.[2] But what emerged, when we tried to put the Hayek theory into our

---

[1] *Treatise on Money*, vol. i, p. 199.
[2] Dennis Robertson's 'Industrial Fluctuation and the Natural Rate of Interest' (*EJ*, 1934)—see above, p. 202—is a particularly distinguished example.

own words, was not Hayek. There was some inner mystery to which we failed to penetrate. We absorbed Hayekian ideas (there are Hayekian influences, not only on Robbins and Robertson, but even on Harrod and Kaldor, for instance, if one looks for them) but there was something central that was missing. It is not so much that it was rejected; it slipped through our fingers. I hope, at long last, to be able to show in this paper what it was.

Hayek himself endeavoured to show us; but I do not think he succeeded. It is indeed true that by the time he made his later efforts, and had got them into print,[1] his audience had dispersed. Keynes had spoken again, with greater clarity; to the opportunities that had been opened up by the *General Theory* what Hayek was saying appeared to have little relevance. It was perhaps again to have relevance, later on; but before that could happen, the 'Revolution' would have to proceed much further on its course.

Let us go back to the beginning, and try to see what it was that had happened. That means going back to Wicksell.

II

In Wicksell, the 'Cumulative Process' is a matter of prices. When the 'market rate' of interest is reduced below the natural rate, prices rise. Nothing is said about the movement of quantities (inputs and outputs). On the bearing of his construction on the causation of Trade Cycles, Wicksell is open-minded.[2]

Hayek was asking the question; what happens to quantities in a Wicksellian cumulative process? He took his model very

[1] *Profits, Interest and Investment* (1939); *Pure Theory of Capital* (1941); 'The Ricardo Effect' (*Economica*, 1942, reprinted in *Individualism and Economic Order*, 1949).

[2] *Lectures on Political Economy*, vol. ii, pp. 209–14. It is interesting that there is the same shift, from an interest in prices to an interest in quantities, between the *Treatise* and the *General Theory*. The *Treatise* is a theory of price-levels; the latter is the *General Theory of Employment*. No wonder that there was this shift in attention, in view of what was happening, contemporaneously, in the real world.

'pure': much purer than Wicksell himself had been accustomed to take it. Prices (all prices) are perfectly flexible, adjusting instantaneously, or as nearly as matters. Price-expectations are not introduced explicitly, for in 1930 their day had not yet come. There must, however, have been some implicit assumption about expectations. We shall hardly go wrong if we take it to be the simplest possible assumption: the 'static' assumption. The same prices as rule today (whatever they are) are expected to continue to rule in the future.

If these assumptions had been strictly maintained, what should have been said about the time-path of the Cumulative Process? When the market rate is reduced below the natural rate, what will happen to the *quantities* of inputs and outputs? The correct answer, on these assumptions, is very simple: the effect will be nil. Prices will rise uniformly; and that is that. When the Wicksell model is taken strictly (as it was being taken strictly), it is in *Neutral equilibrium*. The whole *real* system, of quantities and of *relative* prices, is completely determined by the supply and demand equations in the particular markets; in this *real* system *the* rate of interest is included. There can only be one rate of interest when the markets are in equilibrium; a market rate that is equal to the natural rate. The 'reduction' of the market rate below the natural rate must therefore be interpreted as a disequilibrium phenomenon; a phenomenon that can only persist while the markets are out of equilibrium. As soon as equilibrium is restored, equality between market rate and natural rate must be restored. Thus there is no room for a prolonged discrepancy between market rate and natural rate if there is instantaneous adjustment of prices. Money prices will simply rise *uniformly*; and that is that.

The point is, of course, the same as that which is made in Frisch's famous definition of *dynamics*: consideration of 'the magnitude of certain variables at different points of time' and the introduction of 'equations which embrace at the same time several of these variables belonging to different

instants'.[1] If a system has no lags, so that everything is determined contemporaneously it cannot (endogenously) engender
a process.

Hayek's model does engender a process; some kind of lag
(or lags) must therefore be implicit in it. Where is the lag to
be found? One gets no help from expectational lags, such as
were used by Lindahl;[2] by introducing a lag of price-expectations behind current prices, one can throw the Wicksell
story into a determinate form, but it does not have much
resemblance to the form that Hayek gave it. Nor is it consistent with Hayek's statements to suppose that the lag is
attributable to rigid prices (for instance, wages): an interpretation which was congenial to Robertson,[3] and which
would fit well enough into some versions of Keynesian
theory. A reformulation of the Hayek theory on these lines
does indeed have something to be said for it; we shall be
returning to it later. But it is not what Hayek said. His lag
(for he must have had a lag) is of a different kind.

It is not the production lag (of outputs behind inputs),
the 'period of production' on which he has so much to say.
That also is no help. What is needed is a lag in market
adjustment, of prices behind the demands and supplies of
commodities, or of the demands and supplies behind current prices. If there are no lags in market adjustment, the
time-structure of production is irrelevant to the Cumulative
Process; for there will not be time, before equilibrium is
restored, for the structure of production to be changed.
What then was Hayek's lag?

Consider what happens in the Hayek model. The initial
effect of the expansion of credit—in 'pure' terms, the reduction of the market rate below the natural rate of interest—is
that the money value of Investment rises, implying a rise in
the money prices of producers' goods. We are beginning (it is

---

[1] 'Propagation Problems and Impulse Problems in Dynamic Economics', in *Essays in Honour of Gustav Cassel*, p. 171.
[2] See the discussion in my *Capital and Growth*, pp. 59 ff.
[3] See his 'Hayekian' paper, above quoted.

insisted)[1] from a situation in which there is full employment of labour. Labour is a producers' good; wages are flexible; so the money wage must go up. But what happens about the spending of those wages? Everyone else, at that point in the sequence, would say that here at least there must be an instantaneous, or nearly instantaneous, reaction. The higher wages must be followed, nearly at once—perhaps in the next Robertsonian 'week'—by a rise in the demand for consumption goods.[2] Then, in view of the full employment assumption, the prices of consumption goods must also rise. And there can be no equilibrium of supply and demand, over the whole system, until they have risen enough to withdraw the incentive for the rise in real investment. So (along that channel) we come back to the nil effect, on inputs and out-puts, with which we began.

But Hayek will not allow that. In spite of the rise in wages the demand for consumption goods does not rise; so the prices of consumption goods do not, at this stage, rise. This is how he is able to maintain that there is a rise in the prices of producers' goods, relatively to the prices of consumers' goods, lasting right through the 'boom': the rise on which so much of his argument depends. There has to be a lag of consumption behind wages, which must be large in com-parison with any other lag that is admitted into the system. This is the lag (really, one would think, a most extraordinary lag) which gives the Hayek model its peculiar slant.

Obviously this lag is not acceptable. Yet that is not the end of the Hayek theory. For if one can once get over this step, there is much to be learned from the next stage in the argu-ment, where the effect of this change in relative prices on the 'structure of production' is most carefully worked out. Granted the initial change in the producer-price/consumer-price ratio, and granted that *it can be maintained*, the effect on the production process will be of the kind that Hayek

---

[1] *Prices and Production*, pp. 34–35.
[2] There is no reason, under these assumptions, why there should be any fall in consumption out of profits.

describes. The queer thing about the Hayek theory is not the 'lengthening' and 'shortening' of the 'period of production' which attracted so much attention. It is not the answer that Hayek gives to his question; it is the lack of justification, within the model as set out, for the question being asked at all.

III

It will accordingly be well, before proceeding further, to inquire into the possibility of 'mending' this first step in the Hayek argument: of finding a question, a different question, to which the answer that is given may be a sensible answer.

It is tempting, of course, to try a different lag. Suppose that one keeps the rest of Hayek's assumptions, but instead of the consumption lag, which is so implausible, one introduces a wage-lag: a lag of money wages behind the balance of supply and demand in the market for labour. If there is a lag of this sort (such as Keynes had already implied in the *Treatise*) there can be a rise in producers' good prices relatively to consumers' good prices, such as Hayek requires. And there is room for the phenomenon to which Hayek attributed such importance: that the prices of some producers' goods will rise more than others *as a result of the fall in the rate of interest*. (It must be the fall in the rate of interest which is responsible, for there is nothing else.) Along this route one can incorporate some part of Hayek's work on production structure; and this was an easy way by which a part (though much less than the whole) of Hayek's teaching could be absorbed. But the rigidity (even temporary rigidity) of *money* wages, on which it depends,[1] is a very

---

[1] If money wages are rigid, and there is a credit expansion, the prices of investment goods can still rise. In the production of those investment goods there will be abnormal profits (windfall profits as Keynes had called them). It is quite natural to take it that these windfall profits (or most of them) will be saved; so that a failure of consumption to expand, at this stage, becomes on this assumption quite intelligible. Consumption out of wages fails to expand for one reason; consumption out of profits for another.

un-Hayekian concept; if one pursues this line of thought, one is led towards a theory which is more like that of Keynes, or perhaps of Robertson, than of Hayek.

There is another alternative: at the expense of a more drastic reinterpretation, it enables us to follow in Hayek's footsteps much more exactly.

Suppose that one had *not* started with a 'credit expansion' but had begun with genuine saving, a genuine increase in the propensity to save. The effect of this *in equilibrium* (all I think would now agree) would be a fall in what Wicksell called the natural rate of interest. (Others may prefer other names, but we need not quarrel about that!) Suppose that the market rate of interest is reduced to match, so that demand-supply equilibrium can in fact be maintained. What happens to money prices is quite indeterminate, for (with flexible prices) the equilibrium remains a *neutral equilibrium* in Wicksell's sense; what happens to relative prices, and to quantities, should, however, be determinate. Investment increases (in value terms) relatively to consumption; but since there is, and was, full employment of labour, it is only by 'capital deepening', by 'lengthening of the period of production', that a real shift from consumption to investment can occur. All this just as in Hayek; the fall in the rate of interest is matched by a rise in real wages; whether we like to make the rate of interest (or profit), or the rate of real wages, the king-pin of the argument, is a matter of taste. Whichever we choose, it comes to the same thing.

If we adopt this latter interpretation, we can follow Hayek very closely. We can agree that he was doing something—if it was not what he thought he was doing. The Hayek theory is not a theory of the credit cycle, the *Konjunktur*, which need not work in the way that he describes, nor is it, in fact, at all likely to do so. It is an analysis—a very interesting analysis— of the adjustment of an economy to changes in the rate of genuine saving. In that direction it does make a real contribution. But it is a contribution which, when it was made, was out of due time. It does not belong to the theory of fluctuations, which was the centre of economists' attention in 1930; it is a fore-runner of the growth theory of more recent years. In that application we can still make something of it.

IV

Let us try to follow the further stages of the argument, from this point of view. Let there be an increase in the propensity to save; in order to simplify the argument (but it is not an essential simplification) suppose that it takes the form of a diminished propensity to consume *out of profits*. Let there be a corresponding reduction in the market rate of interest, which (again for simplification) may be supposed to take place so speedily that the price-level of consumption goods can remain unchanged. The fall in the rate of interest will raise the marginal productivity of labour; real wages will therefore rise. But the rise in labour productivity will be greater in those lines of production which are more capital-intensive than in those that are less; in order to restore equality, there must be a shift of labour into more capital-intensive production. That is to say, there will be shift of labour from the production of consumption goods to that of investment goods; but especially into those forms of invest-ment goods production which contribute to processes that, taken as a whole, are more capital-intensive. Let us just say, in order to visualize what is happening, that labour is shifted into the construction of new steel-works and new power-stations. That is just for the picture; the shift can, of course, be expressed in much more complicated forms.

It is an essential (and surely valid) part of Hayek's argu-ment that this shift need not have an immediate effect in diminishing the supply of consumption goods. The current supply is largely a matter of work that has been done in the past; and that has not been changed. If the prices of consump-tion goods are to be kept from rising (as we are supposing) labour must not be taken away from the last stages of consumption goods production; but there will still be opportunities for shift, by taking labour away from earlier stages. Thus what happens, at this point, is that the goods which would have been bought by the receivers of profit (or the equivalents of such goods, for there is no reason why there should not be some redistribution of actual articles) are transferred to provide the increased real wages of labour. And (so far) that is all.

The point must nevertheless come (so Hayek maintains) when the withdrawal of labour from consumption goods production must diminish the supply of consumption goods. A further increase in the saving propensity will then be necessary if the 'boom' (as he would call it) is to be maintained. If this increase is not forthcoming, there will be a 'crisis'.

When the story is interpreted in this manner, though it may not have much relevance to old-style trade crises (which are surely to be interpreted as disequilibrium phenomena, complicated by price- and wage-rigidities and disequilibrium rates of interest, not here allowed for), it does seem possible that it may have relevance in other ways. We are familiar with the ways in which the contrived expansions of our modern planned economies can get into trouble through shortage of saving; the rate of saving which initially seemed adequate to support the expansion proves insufficient to support it at a later stage. One of the reasons why this happens may be the Hayek reason.

I would not myself claim that it is the only reason. The demand for labour, that arises directly out of the expansion programme, does itself very usually have a distinctive time-shape, beginning rather low and rising to a peak some time after the programme has been started. For this reason alone the strain that it sets upon the economy may be deferred. But it is very possible that this strain may be reinforced by the other strain, which Hayek analysed.

Again, it is not *necessary* that there should be a strain of Hayek type. There must, as we have seen, be saving to support the initial investment; but the further saving, needed

to support the supposed fall-off in the supply of consumption
goods, may be so long delayed that it does not have to occur.
The easiest of all sources of labour, to be transferred to the
new processes, is that which was formerly engaged in the
replacement of fixed equipment in the old processes; if for no
other reason, it is this kind of labour which is most likely to
have the right kind of skill. If this labour is transferred, the
normal replacement will have to be delayed; but there will
usually be some replacement which is not very urgent, so
that it can be postponed without serious damage to the
efficiency of production. If the expansion programme is
fairly modest, and if the supply of such dispensable labour is
reasonably abundant, there may be little if any effect upon
the supply of consumption goods, before the products of the
new processes are ready to take over. Thus in an advanced
economy, so long as it is content with modest expansions,
there may not be much reason to be afraid of this 'Hayek
effect', as we may call it. But in the rapid development of the
underdeveloped it can surely be a quite serious danger.

V

In this sense it is possible that there may be a Hayek 'crisis'.
What would it look like if it occurred?

A point has been reached, we suppose, at which the supply
of consumption goods begins to be seriously affected. If the
'boom' is to be maintained, there will have to be a rise in
saving; what is to happen if the propensity to save does not
rise? Only if saving had risen would it be possible to continue
producing in the 'boom' manner, with a low rate of interest
and high real wages. If saving does not rise, this system of
relative prices will be inconsistent with the maintenance of
supply-demand equilibrium in the markets; interest will
have to rise, in order that supply-demand equilibrium should
be maintained—and real wages will have to fall.

Hayek does not simply say that there will be a fall in real
wages; he says that there will be unemployment. But is this

consistent with the price-flexibility which (as we have seen) he must elsewhere be assuming? In order that the fall in real wages (or, more strictly, the fall in the 'real' demand curve for labour) should lead to unemployment, there must be a floor to the real wage that labour will accept; and this must be higher than the real wage which is (now) consistent with full employment. It is not necessary that there should be such a floor at a relevant level; but in order that the (so-called) 'slump' should lead to unemployment something of that sort must be assumed.

One must in any case put out of one's mind the idea that what is involved is a fall in money wages. Real wages may fall because money wages are falling while prices are constant; but they may also fall because of a rise in the prices of consumers' goods, without any fall in money wages. In the present case, as soon as we admit a lag in adjustment (almost any kind of lag), it is the latter of these alternatives which is much the more probable. For it is the *natural* rate of interest which is rising; if there is any lag of the market rate behind it, Wicksell will tell us that prices should have a rising tendency. The Hayek 'slump' is very unlike the slumps of history, since its price-effect goes the wrong way.

It is in its application to deflationary slumps that the Hayek theory is at its worst; and it is a terrible fact that it was in just such conditions—in 1931–2—that it was first propounded. In such conditions its diagnosis was wrong; and its prescription could not have been worse. But because it was wrong then, it does not follow that it must always be wrong. It is possible that there may be conditions to which it is appropriate; and in these days (in 1967) one may not have to look very far before one finds them.

It can happen that there is unemployment even while there is inflation. It can be that labour is insisting on a minimum *real* wage, and that that wage is higher than what is consistent with full employment, whatever happens to prices. Such a condition may arise because of aggressive action by labour unions; but it is in fact more likely to arise when the marginal product of labour, at full employment, has fallen below some customary standard. That again may happen for various reasons; because of capital destruction through war or political upheaval, because of shifts in foreign trade to the country's disadvantage, perhaps because of increasing population; these I suppose are the commonest causes. But it is by no means excluded that it should happen for Hayek's reason: in the aftermath of an attempted expansion, greater than the economy was able, or willing, to afford—so that it has been abortive. If shortages develop from such a cause, prices will rise; in Wicksell's terms, from a rise in the natural rate of interest. Prices being flexible, and quickly reacting—it is very reasonable to suppose that in these conditions they will be quickly reacting—there may be no rate of price-rise which will not be altogether explosive, unless so severe a hand is kept upon the monetary circulation that unemployment results. There may be rapid inflation; but if it is to be kept down to a finite rate of inflation, there must be unemployment. This is the Hayek 'slump'. To such conditions the Keynesian prescription is irrelevant, as irrelevant as Hayek's was in 1931. Hayek's prescription— the direction of policy towards the restoration of the marginal productivity of labour to a normal level, as soon as possible, but with a realization that it cannot be done immediately— will then after all be right.

INDEX

PRINTED IN GREAT BRITAIN
AT THE UNIVERSITY PRESS, OXFORD
BY VIVIAN RIDLER
PRINTER TO THE UNIVERSITY